University
Writing Course

John Morley – Peter Doyle – Ian Pople

Express Publishing

Published by Express Publishing

**Liberty House, Greenham Business Park, Newbury,
Berkshire RG19 6HW, United Kingdom
Tel: (0044) 1635 817 363 - Fax: (0044) 1635 817 463
email: inquiries@expresspublishing.co.uk
www.expresspublishing.co.uk**

First published 2007
Sixth impression 2016

Made in the EU

ISBN: 978-1-84679-366-0

Acknowledgements

We would like to thank colleagues at the University of Manchester for their
suggestions and input into these materials, in particular: Pat Campbell and Bill
Guariento for piloting some of the early versions of this material.

Thanks to all the staff at Express Publishing who have contributed their skills to
producing this book. Thanks for their support and patience are due in particular
to: Megan Lawton (Editor in Chief), Julie Baker Todd (senior editor), Steve Blake
(editorial assistant), Richard White (senior production controller), the Express
design team, and Tony Mason, David Smith and Timothy Forster.

We would also like to acknowledge all those who have allowed us to use
material in this publication. A full list may be found in the bibliography on
page 109.

Contents

Preface

This book has been written for current and prospective students of English speaking universities whose first language is not English. It is aimed at the large group of students, undergraduate and postgraduate, whose level in English may be at or around level 6 in IELTS or 560 (PBT) in TOEFL, and who still need to further refine and improve their academic writing. Adopting a general English for academic purposes approach, the units cover a broad range of key functional and textual areas. Each unit includes a range of authentic sample texts, controlled and less controlled writing exercises, and a reference list of useful phrases. The materials have been developed over a period of 10 years at the University of Manchester by authors with a total of over 40 years experience of teaching academic writing in a University environment.

John Morley
Peter Doyle
Ian Pople

I. ORGANISING INFORMATION

The basic units of organisation in a written text are paragraphs. A paragraph normally contains several sentences which are all concerned with one main idea (or topic). In a well-written paragraph, the main idea (or topic) is expressed in a topic sentence, which is usually (but not always) the first sentence. The other sentences in the paragraph develop the main idea in some way. The whole paragraph should be coherent and easy to follow.

1 Introductory exercise on paragraph development
In the text below identify the topic sentence and reorder the sentences to form the original paragraph.

a		Finally, as the traditional means of communicating knowledge internationally, journals are accepted and recognised by scholars and researchers. They define what is important, maintain standards and also help to create an invisible college of those concerned with a topic.
b		They use technologies which are available to virtually every nation and to most academic institutions, regardless of age or level of development.
c		Through a well-established international infrastructure of library acquisition, new journals can reach concerned scholarly audiences fairly efficiently.
d		Journals have significant advantages as a means of international scholarly communication. They are relatively inexpensive.

2 Focus on paragraph development

The above paragraph has a typical structure that can be identified in many paragraphs: the topic sentence introduces the new idea, topic, argument or piece of information into the main text. This is then either explained further or supported by subsequent sentences. This structure can be represented like this:

> Topic Sentence
>
> (new idea, expressed in general terms)
>
> Explanatory or Supporting Information (may include):
>
> explanation
>
> and/or   past research
>
> "   illustrations/examples
>
> "   quotations
>
> "   statistics
>
> "   specific aspects

It is important for the unity of a paragraph that the explanatory or supporting information should directly relate to the topic sentence and that only one main idea should be discussed. A new main idea should be treated in a separate paragraph. It is also important that the explanatory or supporting information should not repeat the general idea expressed in the topic sentence.

3 Exercises on paragraph development
The sentences in the boxes below (i-iv) are not in order. First, identify the topic sentence and then put the remaining sentences in order.

(i)

a		Britain lost most of its Empire after World War II, but even as the sun was setting on the Empire, the United States was simultaneously rising as a political, economic and military superpower. Thus the spread of English has continued without a break.
b		The widespread use of English and its current position as the world language is not accidental, nor it is attributable to any intrinsic linguistic superiority of English as a language.
c		Wherever the British acquired colonies, they brought English with them as the language of administration.
d		It began with the establishment of the British Empire in the eighteenth and nineteenth centuries.

(ii)

a		Historically, this is because new foods and new ways of processing and cooking foods have arisen since the separation of the two nations.
b		The many differences in the terminology of transportation result from the fact that the railroad (British: *railway*) and motor industries developed after the separation of the United States and Great Britain.
c		The vagaries* of fashion have caused divergence in the vocabulary of clothing.
d		Three broad semantic areas in which British-American lexical differences are especially noticeable are food, clothing and transportation.

* = unexpected, unpredictable changes

(iii)

a		When a college student says that a certain book is *great*, it is more than likely that the statement has nothing to do with the value of the book judged as a work of art but simply means that he or she thoroughly enjoyed it.
b		By *extension of meaning* is meant the widening of a word's signification until it covers much more than the idea originally conveyed.
c		A box of candy or a chair may be *lovely*, and anything from a ball game to the weather may be *great*.
d		The word *lovely*, for example, means primarily worthy to be loved, and *great* means large in size, the opposite of small. But today *lovely* and *great* have no such meanings.

(iv)	a		Cycling alters the anatomical position of the spine (to a flexed position), particularly the thoracic spine, and exposes the anterior portion of the vertebral column to higher compression.
	b		Among cyclists, however, the most potentially serious of these disorders might be increased thoracic curvature.
	c		Children may become interested in competitive sport at an early age.
	d		Early involvement (prior to maturity) in competitive sports often exposes individuals to types of stress that may affect their growth, producing a disruption of the normal growth pattern (Frost, 1979; Watkins, 1999).

4 Exercise on dividing a text into paragraphs
In the following text the paragraph divisions are not indicated. Identify the topic sentence(s) and divide the text into paragraphs. There are three paragraphs in the original text.

Weather conditions in Saudi Arabia vary almost as much as the terrain. In the mountains that fringe the peninsula on the west, south and southeast, annual rainfall is about 50 centimetres and there are often torrential downpours and destructive flash floods; yet parts of the Rub' al-Khali may receive no rain for as long as 10 years. Over much of central, northern and
5   northeastern Arabia, average annual rainfall is 5 to 15 centimetres and highly variable from year to year. Temperature and humidity ranges are equally disparate. In the interior the air is dry, while on the coasts, summer humidity is excessive, particularly at night. In summer, temperatures in some areas may reach 50° C (122° F) in the shade, but in spring, the days are balmy and the nights are clear. In winter, temperatures drop below freezing in the central and
10   northern regions, and snow sometimes falls in the mountains, the northern plateau and even in the capital Riyadh. There are also strong winds, such as the prevailing northwest winds along the eastern coast – the winds called the *shamal* – which frequently whip up dust and sandstorms. The climate of the peninsula, nevertheless, is largely characterised by aridity and heat. As a result, the vegetation, wildlife and domesticated animals of the peninsula share one
15   distinctive feature: a high degree of adaptation to the special demands of life in the desert. The ability of men to adapt and survive in this harsh environment has had important effects on the history of the peninsula and Saudi Arabia.

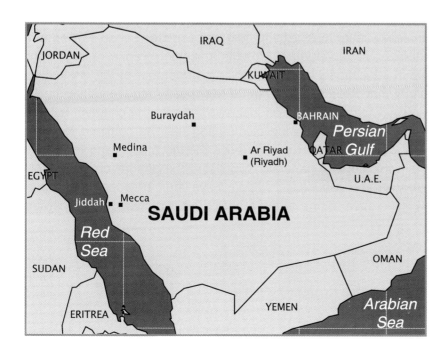

Figure 1.1. Map of Saudi Arabia and surrounding areas

II. GIVING EXAMPLES

5 **Pre-reading**

(i) • **Why do writers give examples in their texts?**
   • **In what position in a paragraph would you normally expect to find examples?**

(ii) • **Do you know any words in English whose meanings have changed with time?**
   • **How have they changed?**

6 **Reading for main points**
Read the extract below and note two ways in which the meaning of a word can change and give one example of each.

(1) It has been observed that in their sense development, words often pursue certain well-marked tendencies. Among the more common of these are *extension* of meaning and *narrowing* of meaning. By *extension of meaning* is meant the widening of a word's signification until it covers much more than the idea originally conveyed. The tendency is sometimes called
5 *generalisation*. The word *lovely*, for example, means primarily worthy to be loved, and *great* means large in size, the opposite of small. But today *lovely* and *great* have no such meaning. A box of candy or a chair may be *lovely*, and anything from a ball game to the weather may be *great*. When a college student says that a certain book is *great*, it is more than likely that the statement has nothing to do with the value of the book judged as a work of art, but simply means
10 that he or she thoroughly enjoyed it. In everyday use these words have come to express only enthusiastic approval of a rather vague sort. Another illustration is the word *dean*. It has, of course, its proper meanings, such as the head of the chapter in a cathedral church or the head of the faculty in a college. But it has come to be used as a designation for the senior or foremost person of any group or class, so that we may speak of the *dean* of American critics, or, indeed,
15 of sportswriters.

(2) The opposite tendency is for a word gradually to acquire a more restricted sense, or to be chiefly used in one special connection. A classic example of this practice is the word *doctor*. There are doctors (i.e., learned men) in theology, law and many other fields beside medicine, but nowadays when we send for *the* doctor we mean a member of only one profession. In some
20 of the preceding paragraphs, especially those in which were presented examples of old words with new meanings, will be found a number of similar instances. The verb *to park* as applied to automobiles and the war word *tank* are cases in point. The use of a word in a restricted sense does not preclude its use also in other meanings. Often the restricted sense of a word belongs to a special or class vocabulary. An *enlargement* means to a photographer a large print made
25 from a small negative, and in educational circles a *senior* is a member of the graduating class. Consequently, it sometimes happens that the same word will acquire different restricted meanings for different people. The word *gas* is an inclusive term for the chemist, but it calls up a more restricted idea in the kitchen. Narrowing of meaning may be confined to one locality under the influence of local conditions. *Nickel* in America means a coin, and for a number of
30 years the word *prohibition* in this country generally suggested the prohibition of alcohol. In the same way the terms *democrat* and *republican* seldom have their broader significance to an American but rather imply adherence to one or the other of the two chief political parties in the United States.

7 **Guided summary**
Below is a short summary of the text. However, a number of important words and phrases have been removed. Can you complete the summary by filling in the gaps?

With time, there is a tendency for some words to **1)** .... their meaning and for **2)** .... to acquire a more restricted meaning. An **3)** .... of the former is the word **4)** ...., which originally meant large in size but can now mean **5)** .... The word *doctor* is a good example of the latter. Originally meaning **6)** .... man, nowadays it is usually **7)** .... to refer to a medical practitioner.

8 **Language focus**
• Read through the text again and underline any language used to introduce examples.
• What other words or phrases can be used to give examples?

9 **Reading for detail**
Now re-read the text and complete the table below.

Paragraph 1

Extension of meaning

       Example 1:   Word lovely   New meaning vague approval

       Example 2:   Word ....   New meaning ....

       Example 3:   Word ....   New meaning ....

Paragraph 2

Narrowing of meaning

       Example 1:   Word ....   New meaning ....

       Example 2:   Word ....   New meaning ....

       Example 3:   Word ....   New meaning ....

Narrowing of meaning (special vocabulary)

       Example 1:   Word ....   New meaning ....

       Example 2:   Word ....   New meaning ....

       Example 3:   Word ....   New meaning ....

Narrowing of meaning (local vocabulary)

       Example 1:   Word ....   New meaning ....

       Example 2:   Word ....   New meaning ....

       Example 3:   Word ....   New meaning ....

       Example 4:   Word ....   New meaning ....

How are the examples of special and local vocabulary introduced?

(10) Language for giving examples

Examples as the main information in a sentence

| For example,
For instance, | the word *doctor* used to mean a learned man. |

| A good
A classic
A well-known
A typical
Another | example of this is the word *doctor*. |

| Examples of extension of meaning | are
include | *lovely* and *great*. |

The following are examples of extension of meaning: *lovely* and *great*.

| The word *lovely* is a good | example
illustration | of extension of meaning. |

Extension of meaning can be illustrated by the words *lovely* and *great*.

| The word *doctor* | illustrates this point.
shows this point clearly. |

| The word *doctor* | is a case in point.
is a good example of this.
serves as a good illustration of this. |

Words such as *lovely* and *great* serve as good examples.

| This | is exemplified
is shown
is illustrated | by the words *lovely* and *great*. |

Examples as additional information in a sentence

Pavlov found that if some other stimulus, for example the ringing of a bell, preceded the food, the dog would start salivating.

A number of well-known diseases can result at least in part from stress, including arthritis, asthma, migraine, headaches and ulcers.

In Paris, Gassendi kept in close contact with many other prominent scholars such as Kepler, Galileo, Hobbes and Descartes.

| The prices of resources, | such as
like | copper, iron ore, oil, coal and aluminium, have declined in real terms over the past 20 years. |

11 Sentence constructions using *for example* and *such as*
- **What kind of grammatical structures follow** *for example* **and** *such as***?**
- **Is there any difference between them?**

(i) **Rewrite the sentences (a-f) below so that they include the examples which are given on the right. Use** *such as* **and make whatever changes you feel are necessary.**
Example: *The desire to avoid stress may also lead people to avoid potentially beneficial changes to their lives, such as job changes and promotions.*

(ii) **Rewrite the examples on the right as complete sentences using** *for example***. Expand on the information which is given.**
Example: *For example, they may avoid changing jobs or fail to pursue promotion opportunities.*

Sentences	Examples
a The desire to avoid stress may also lead people to avoid potentially beneficial changes to their lives.	**i** job changes, promotions
b Giving people the correct information can encourage them to adopt health promoting behaviour.	**ii** cutting down on smoking cutting down on drinking
c People are more likely to pay attention to certain bodily sensations when they are under stress.	**iii** aches, pains
d The focus of medical care in our society has been shifting towards changing many of our unhealthy behaviours rather than simply curing the resulting diseases.	**iv** poor eating habits, smoking, failure to exercise
e For some people, being called upon to give a talk in front of a class is a highly stressful stimulus that will immediately produce symptoms of an alarm reaction.	**v** a pounding heart and a dry mouth
f Young people begin smoking for a variety of reasons.	**vi** peer pressure and the role modelling of parents

12 **Writing Tasks**

(i) **Choose one or more of the points below and write a paragraph, adding examples to support the point(s).**

- Clothing for traditional weddings varies from culture to culture.
- Differences in men's and women's speech may be partly based on social factors.
- What is described as preventative medicine may cover a number of different practices.
- Smoking has many disadvantages. Some of them concern personal hygiene and appearance whereas more serious disadvantages relate to health.

(ii) **Write one or two paragraphs illustrating a fact, theory or argument within your own subject area.**

(1) Pre-reading
- **What is a mineral?**
- *Do you know which minerals are found in the body?*
- *Do you know which minerals are good for the body and which are not?*

(2) Reading
Read the text below and note how trace minerals are classified.

(1) Scientists first started to analyse the chemicals in the body at the beginning of the twentieth century. However, their equipment was not sensitive enough to accurately measure all the chemicals they found. Therefore, when scientists detected a particular mineral in the body but could not find enough to measure, they called it a 'trace' mineral. Thus the official definition of

5   a trace mineral is one that makes up less than 0.01% (1/10,000th part) of the total body weight.

(2) The trace minerals group comprises over fifty chemical elements. It is divided into three categories on the basis of how useful the minerals are to the body. The first category is 'essential' trace minerals, which are necessary in a person's diet for that person to be fully healthy. These minerals include nine known to be vital for full health: zinc, copper, selenium,

10   chromium, manganese, molybdenum, iodine, fluoride and cobalt, in that order.

(3) The second category of trace minerals are 'toxic' trace minerals. These are minerals that cause toxicity problems when there is too much of any of them in the body because, for example, there is too much of them in the environment. The particular elements in this category may change from time to time, and include three of the minerals in the first category (arsenic,

15   cadmium and lead) that the body actually needs in very small quantities. However, they become toxic when they are present in the body above certain levels. Other such minerals are mercury and tin.

(4) The third class of non-essential trace minerals is everything else. These are all the other minerals that are present in the body but not essential in the diet and not thought to have any

20   particular purpose. Thus these minerals do not cause any concern over toxicity or deficiency.

(3) Guided summary
Below is a short summary of the text you have just read. Complete the summary by filling in the gaps.

The official definition of a trace mineral is that it **1)** .... up less than 0.01% of the **2)** .... body weight. One way of **3)** .... trace minerals is according to how **4)** .... they are to the body. Although some of these minerals belong to more than **5)** .... category, most minerals can be placed into one of three **6)** .... These are **7)** .... , **8)** .... and **9)** ....

4 **Sentence construction**
Look at the following sentence:

| On the basis of
According to | how harmful they are to the body, trace minerals may be divided
into essential, toxic and non-essential. |

Now make up similar sentences from the columns in the box below:

a	GNP per capita	the education system	deciduous and evergreen trees
b	their physical appearance	animals	the primary sector, the secondary sector and the tertiary sector
c	age of study	countries	Negroids, Caucasians and Mongoloids
d	whether they eat plants, other animals or both	human beings	low-income countries, middle-income countries and high-income countries
e	whether or not they shed their leaves seasonally	rocks	herbivores, carnivores and omnivores
f	origin	broad-leaved trees	igneous rocks, sedimentary rocks and metamorphic rocks

5 **Sentence level gap-fill exercise**
a) Use these words/phrases to fill in the gaps in the following sentences.

may be divided into   on the basis of   such as   including

i A number of the developing countries **1)** .... energy exporters, **2)** .... the OPEC countries, and energy importers, **3)** .... some other 'middle income' countries.

ii The costs of children **4)** .... direct costs, **5)** .... the expenditure on the baby and mother around the time of birth, and indirect costs **6)** .... the earnings lost by mothers who take time out of paid employment, and who may return to work part-time and at lower rates of pay.

iii 7) .... their age and a test performance, any new children can then be given a test score which reflects their performance relative to the national average.

b) Use the following words/phrases to fill in the gaps in the following sentences.

third group   comprises   divided into   main groups
on the basis of   second category   further sub-divided into   tiny

i Medical teachers in Britain can be classified into three **1)** .... : a **2)** .... minority who are trained in educational theory and methods and who often are not medically qualified themselves, a **3)** .... consisting of staff holding official 'teaching' appointments but without formal teacher training, and a **4)** .... of NHS doctors who teach, and which **5)** .... most NHS doctors.

ii 6) .... their legal status, private companies may be **7)** .... limited and unlimited companies and private limited companies can be **8)** .... those limited by shares and those limited by guarantee.

6 **Text restructuring**
See if you can reorder the information in the text below into two logical and coherent paragraphs. Give reasons for your ordering.

Figure 2.1. A barred spiral galaxy

a		Regular galaxies were divided into ellipticals and spirals.
b		His scheme, published in 1936, is based on an examination of photographs taken by Mt Wilson's 1.5 and 4.5 meter telescopes.
c		Other schemes have been developed, but Hubble's basic classification is still the most widely used.
d		Edwin Hubble's effort to classify the 'extragalactic nebulae', as he called galaxies, was a lifelong pursuit.
e		Hubble divided galaxies into two broad types: regulars, which show rotational symmetry about a central nucleus, and irregulars which lack this symmetry, and thus were not included in this sequence.
f		As his collection of photographs grew, he modified the scheme but kept its essential features.
g		Two branches of spirals – one with a bar across the nucleus – were classified according to the size of the nuclear region and the openness of the arms.

Figure 2.2. A spiral galaxy

7 **Language for classifying**

General classifications

X may be divided into	Xi and Xii.	
	three main	sub-groups. classes.

| X may be classified | on the basis of according to depending on in terms of | Y | into Xi and Xii. |

On the basis of Y, X may be divided into Xi and Xii.

X may be sub-divided according to whether or not there is Y.

Xi may be further divided into Xi(a) and Xi(b).

| Within the | group zone | classified as X, there are four variations: |

Within each sub-class, there are a number of variations of ...

| X | is made up of consists of comprises | Xi and Xii. |

Specific classifications

| In the U.S. system, X is graded | according to whether ... on the basis of ... |

| Smith | divided grouped | X's into two broad types: Xi's and Xii's. |

| Later researchers sub-divided the two categories into Xi and Xii and Yi and Yii | according to the extent of ... on the basis of ... |

Thomas and Nelson (1996) describe four basic types of validity: logical, content, criterion and construct.

8 **Vocabulary**
   a) The following words are used for classifying. You have read or used some of them already.
   - Decide what part of speech they are, e.g. *noun*, *adjective*, or *verb*.
   - Decide which of them are formal and can be used in academic writing and which are informal and should not be used in academic writing,
     e.g. *pigeonhole – noun and verb – informal*

a	category	**d**	classify	**g**	pigeonhole	**j**	set
b	class	**e**	distinguish	**h**	place	**k**	sort out
c	system	**f**	grouping	**i**	separate	**l**	stereotype

b) Choose from the following words to fill the gaps.

category   classify   distinguish   stereotype   system

i   Music reviewers love to **1)** .... performers, but Jocelyn Pook has a distinct personality all of her own.

ii Many biographies fall into the **2)** .... which might be described as scholarly but not academic. They are written by professional writers for an educated reader rather than for the smaller market of academic specialists in a particular subject.

iii The Education Minister urged schools not to **3)** .... pupils from certain racial groups as troublemakers.

c) Use the following words to fill the gaps in the sentences.

a set of   distinction   grouping   selected   distinguish

i   A preliminary **1)** .... may be based on the **2)** .... between water soluble and water insoluble soils.

ii Naturopathic remedies tend to be derived from the natural world and are **3)** .... and administered according to **4)** .... basic principles.

iii South Africa's conservation efforts have received a great deal of publicity and it has been difficult to **5)** .... myth from reality.

(9) Listing

When writers classify, they may well need to list their classifications. They will often use words such as: *categories*, *classes* and *groupings*.

Some other words are – *advantages, aspects, causes, consequences, criticisms, effects, elements, examples, factors, features, objectives, points, reasons, stages, trends* and *varieties*.

a) Now use three of the following five words to fill the gaps in these sentences.

advantages   consequences   elements   features   objectives

i   US currency has traditionally had a number of **1)** .... that deter counterfeiters. One is the cotton and linen paper, which has a distinctive feel. Another is the ink on the notes which is manufactured according to secret formulas.

ii Extreme fatigue may result in several **2)** ....: firstly, people may limit their exercise to stop pain and discomfort; secondly, there will a lessening in social interaction; thirdly, quality of life will lessen; and, finally, mental depression may increase.

iii Animals gather in herds because it gives them three **3)** ....: information about the presence of potential rivals, the assistance of other males in collective defence of the herd; and a reduced likelihood of any particular herd being chosen for attack.

b) Look at sentences i, ii and iii in a) again. What other words and phrases in the sentences are used for listing?

c) Now use three of the following five words to fill in the gaps in these sentences.

causes   consequences   elements   objectives   stages

i   Scientists studying two big craters on Earth have found two particular **1)** ....: one was created by the impact of a comet while the other was the result of the impact of an asteroid.

ii Jazz is often characterised as having three key **2)** ....: first, 'swing' – it makes you want to tap your feet; second, 'improvisation' – the players often invent the melodies as they go; third, 'individual voices' – the major musicians in jazz history, for example, Louis Armstrong and John Coltrane, had their own style and sound.

iii Stopping smoking is increasingly described as a process with three distinct **3)** ....: smokers become motivated to change, they decide to change, and finally, they manage to change.

d) Look at sentences i, ii and iii in b) again. What words and phrases in the sentences are used for listing?

10 **Language for Listing**

a Numbering

1 Exact numbers with countable nouns:

$$X \text{ has } three/five \quad \begin{array}{l} \text{advantages:} \\ \text{functions:} \\ \text{aspects:} \end{array}$$

2 Inexact numbers with countable nouns:

$$X \text{ has } several/some/a \ number \ of/many \quad \begin{array}{l} \text{advantages:} \\ \text{functions:} \\ \text{aspects:} \end{array}$$

Note that a countable noun is followed by a colon (:) if/when a list follows.

b Sequencing

Numbering can be followed by sequence words:

- firstly, secondly, etc.
- lastly, finally, etc.
- one, next, then, also, another, too, further, etc.

c Other types of sequencing

1 Grammatical parallelism

Note the use of the same verb forms here.

There are *two* advantages to be derived from X: *it enables* Y and *it makes* Z possible.

2 Lexical repetition

Note the repeated vocabulary here.

The following are some of the principal internal economies of scale: *economies* in the factors of production, *economies* in administration, marketing *economies* and other *economies* of large scale.

11 **a) Now rewrite the following passage using some of the listing strategies you have just looked at. In your rewriting use the word** *'functions'*.

Political parties in the Western political system have ideologies and political programmes. They also articulate the interests of society and try to influence ruling bodies. They try to make citizens more politically active. They recruit candidates and form governments.

b) Now rewrite the following passage, adapted from the newspaper, *USA Today*, **so that it uses the words** *'risk'* **and** *'factors'*.

If parents want to reduce the chances that their teenagers will use drugs, alcohol or tobacco, they should keep three rules in mind: Do not let teenagers get too stressed, make sure they stay busy and do not give them too much spending money.

12 **Writing Tasks**
a) Write a short text describing the main types and functions of food. The outline below might help you:

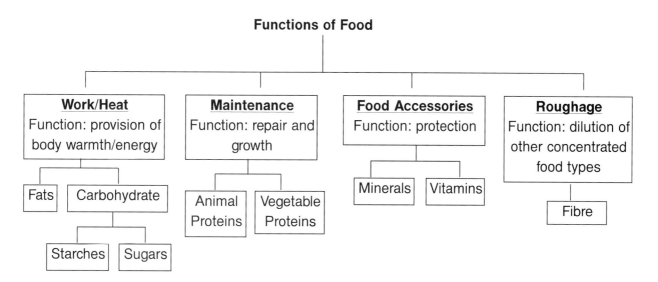

b) Write a short text classifying one of the following:
- the different types of schools in your country;
- the different kinds of television programmes in your country;
- the different types of music in your country;
- the different forms of communication that we use.

1 Pre-reading

(i) • Why do academic writers define things?
  • What kind of terms does an academic writer usually need to define?
  • Are definitions given in dictionaries appropriate for academic writing?
  • Can different writers define the same thing in different ways?

(ii) • Can you think of a short definition for the word *grammar*? Compare your definition with those of other students.

2 Reading
Now read the text below. How many definitions of grammar can you find?

(1) It is difficult to capture the central role played by grammar in the structure of language, other than by using a metaphor such as 'framework' or 'skeleton'. But no physical metaphor can express satisfactorily the multifarious kinds of formal patterning and abstract relationships that are brought to light in a grammatical analysis.

5 **(2)** Two steps can usually be distinguished in the study of grammar. The first step is to identify units in the stream of speech (or writing or signing) - units such as 'word' or 'sentence'. The second step is to analyse the patterns into which these units fall, and the relationship of meaning that these patterns convey. Depending on which units we recognise at the beginning of the study, so the definition of grammar alters. Most approaches begin by recognising the 'sentence',
10 and grammar is thus most widely defined as 'the study of sentence structure'. The grammar of a language, from this point of view, is an account of the language's possible sentence structures, [which is] organised according to certain general principles. For example, in the opening pages of the most influential grammatical treatise of recent times, the American linguist Noam Chomsky (1928 -) writes that a grammar is a 'device of some sort for producing the sentences
15 of the language under analysis' (1957, p.11).

3 Language focus
Write out the definitions of grammar in the text by completing these sentences, then make notes/discuss how the three definitions differ grammatically.

a Most approaches begin by recognising the 'sentence', and grammar is ....
....

b A grammar of a language, from this point of view, ...
....

c Noam Chomsky (1928 -) writes that ....
....

4 Gap-fill and analysis exercise with different types of definitions
Write in the missing words using the information given in the definitions. Share your answers with the rest of the class.

a A .... is an institution where knowledge is 'produced' and passed on to others.

b .... is a systematic process which consists of three elements or components: (1) a question, problem, or hypothesis, (2) data, and (3) analysis and interpretation of data.

c The .... is the full collection of all the computers [which are] linked to the Internet which hold documents that are mutually accessible through the use of a standard protocol (the Hyper Text Transfer Protocol, or http).

d A .... is a word which can occur as the subject or object of a verb or the object of a preposition, can be modified by an adjective, and can be limited by a determiner.

e .... may broadly be defined as the scientific study of the celestial bodies, their motion, relative positions and nature.

f .... Economics may be defined as the branch of economics [which is] concerned with the measurement, causes and consequences of social problems.

g A .... is the largest unit of grammatical organisation within which grammatical classes (nouns, verbs, adverbs) are said to function.

h .... is the branch of geology which studies ancient life. It is the essential tool of the stratigrapher for purposes of correlation, strata identification, establishment of sequences and determination of environments. From a biological point of view, palaeontology yields important evidence for evolution and adaptation of organisms to different environments.

- **Re-read the definitions. What are the grammatical differences? Pay particular attention to verb forms and the use of articles and relative pronouns.**
- **What is a typical structure for a one-sentence definition?**
- **How does definition h) differ from the others?**

5 **Sentence construction exercise**
Write definitions using the words and phrases in the table below. Add articles, extra words and the verb in brackets in the active or passive. Where the verb is passive, leave out the relative pronoun *which + is/are*. Where the verb is active, reduce the structure by adding *-ing* to the verb, when it refers to a continuous state or a current activity.

electron	gaseous envelope	usually (determine) by the test-retest method, where the first measure is compared to a second or third measure under the same conditions.
antigen	measure of the consistency or reproducibility of data	(infect) plants and animals, usually manifesting their presence by causing disease. They are unable to multiply outside the host tissues.
atmosphere	elementary particle	(cause) the formation of antibodies, the body's natural response to foreign substances.
statistics	substance	(refer to) the study of the classes of words, their inflections, and their functions and relations in a sentence.
reliability	branch of mathematics	(assume) to be a constituent of every atom. It contains the smallest known electric charge.
virus	term	(surround) the Earth or other celestial body.
grammar	member of a group of sub-microscopic agents	(concern) with the collection, analysis, interpretation and presentation of masses of numerical data.

a (electron) ....
....

b (antigen) ....

....

c (atmosphere) ....

....

d (statistics) ....

....

e (reliability) ....

....

....

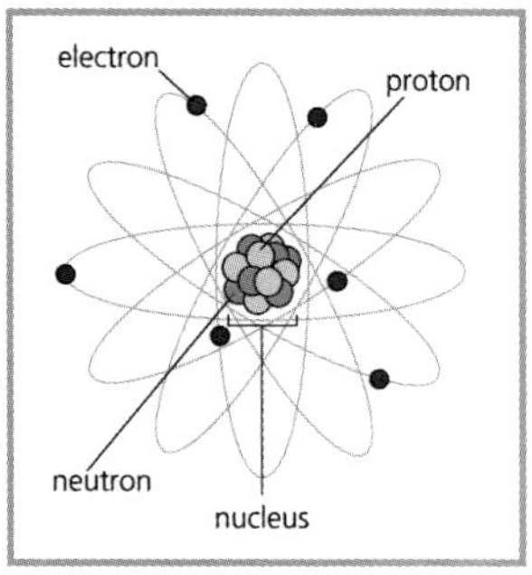

f (virus) ....

....

g (grammar) ....

....

Figure 3.1. An atom is the smallest unit of matter that has the characteristic properties of a chemical element.

6 **Text study (i)**
In what ways is the function of the text below different from that of the text studied in Ex. 2?

It was Chomsky (1965) who gave prominence to the competence - performance distinction (although the theoretical distinction between the terms was not Chomsky's). For Chomsky, 'competence' refers to mastery of the principles governing language behaviour. 'Performance' refers to the manifestation of the internalised rules in actual language use. The terms have come
5 to be used to refer to what a person knows about language (competence) and what a person does (performance). More recently, the term 'communicative competence' has gained currency. This refers to the knowledge of the rules of use and appropriacy and includes linguistic competence. While this might seem reasonably straightforward, there are a number of complicating factors. To begin with, there is nothing like universal agreement on what is meant
10 by 'knowing'. Does 'knowing the rules of language' mean being able to recite them? If so, most native speakers must be classed as incompetent.

- **What structures have been used to write about Chomsky's definitions in this text and the text in Ex. 2?**
- **What other ways are there of introducing other people's definitions?**

Text study (ii)
The text below, taken from a post-graduate dissertation, illustrates the complexity of many academic definitions. How many definitions of 'poverty' can you identify?

(1) Our understanding of poverty has come a long way since its initial conception as 'a lack of the minimum nutritional intake needed to sustain life' (Fowler, 1997: 3). Chambers *et al.* (1991) identify two senses of the word poverty. Its broader meaning is a synonym for deprivation. The second sense refers to what is measured in poverty assessment. Whereas the former helps
5   understand poverty as a basis for designing interventions, the latter is needed to give an overview of poverty, to target the poor, and to judge interventionists' impacts.

(2) A further distinction can be made between absolute and relative poverty. Absolute poverty occurs when individuals or households are not able to meet their basic needs, e.g. food and shelter, or their survival needs, e.g. education and healthcare. We must, however, recognise that
10 poverty depends on the particular society. An individual suffers from relative poverty when 'they lack the resources to obtain the types of diets, participate in the activities and have the living conditions and amenities which are customary, or at least widely accepted and approved, in the societies to which they belong' (Townsend, 1979: 31).

(3) A third division is between traditional definitions, based on a narrow income/consumption
15 view, and more recent definitions, which have broadened to include physical assets (e.g. land and water), human capital (e.g. health and education) and human rights (e.g. dignity and political freedom). The World Bank and other development actors now accept that poverty encompasses these, and other forms of deprivation, such as vulnerability, exposure to risk, voicelessness and powerlessness (World Bank, 2000/2001). This inclusion of a lack of choice or
20 capability to take a full part in human society was proposed by Amartya Sen (1999), and deepens our understanding of the realities of poverty.

(4) A final distinction deserves consideration here. Whereas an income based poverty profile identifies poverty at one point in time, many households move in and out of poverty, e.g. seasonally. A dynamic approach to defining poverty will therefore be more insightful, as is
25 captured by the notion of vulnerability (Hanmer *et al.*, 1997). The transient poor, who move in and out of poverty, should be distinguished from those in chronic poverty, i.e. those 'who either experience extended duration of poverty, or those who benefit the least and/or suffer the most from contemporary development policies and practices, and for whom emergence from poverty is most difficult' (Okidi and McKay, 2003).

- **Now re-read the text and complete the table below.**

Paragraph 1 **Heading:** Initial definitions of poverty

1 Fowler (1997:3): ....
....

2 Chambers *et al.* (1991) i: ....
....

3 Chambers *et al.* (1991) ii: ....
....

Paragraph 2 **Heading:** _____

1 Absolute poverty: ....
....

2 Relative poverty: ....
....

Paragraph 3 **Heading:** _____

1 Traditional definitions: ....
....

2 More recent definitions: ....
....

3 World Bank (2000/2001): ....
....

Paragraph 4 **Heading:** _____

1 Transient poverty: ....
....

2 Chronic poverty: ....
....

- **What is the writer's own attitude to the various definitions?**

Simple definitions

A university is an institution where ...

Sociology may be broadly defined as the study of ...

A grammar of a language is an account of ...

An electron is an elementary particle [which is] assumed to be a constituent of every atom.

General meanings/application of meanings

The term 'performance' has come to be used to refer to ...

The term 'performance' is generally understood to mean ...

The term 'English for Specific Purposes' has been applied to situations where students ...

Specifying terms that are used in an essay/thesis

In this essay the term 'overseas student' will be used in its broadest sense to refer to all students who ...

Throughout this thesis, the term 'education' is used to refer to informal systems as well as formal systems.

For the purposes of this essay, 'development policy' will be defined as ...

Indicating difficulties with definitions

A generally accepted definition of 'poverty' is lacking.

It is difficult to define 'poverty' precisely.

It is difficult to give a precise definition of 'poverty'.

The problem with this definition of 'poverty' is that it ...

Referring to other people's definitions

Noam Chomsky (1928 -) writes that a grammar is ...

The term 'performance' is used by Chomsky to refer to ...

Chomsky uses the term 'performance' to refer to ...

For Smith (1997), 'poverty' means/refers to ...

Jones (1997: 3) defines 'poverty' as '...'

According to Jones (1997: 3) poverty is '...'

'Poverty' is defined by Smith (1997: 3) as '...'

Poverty will be understood in the sense of Jones (1997: 3), namely as '...'

The definition of poverty by Smith (1997: 3) will be adopted: '...'

8 **Writing Tasks**

a) Write a one-paragraph definition of your academic subject or one of the sub-branches of your subject, or the field of research you are engaged in.

b) Read the following text and then write one-sentence summaries of Lock's (1996) definitions of formal and functional grammar.

There are many ways of describing the grammar of a language. One approach sees grammar as a set of *rules* which specify all the possible grammatical structures of the language. In this approach, a clear distinction is usually made between grammatical (sometimes called *well-formed*) sentences and ungrammatical sentences. The primary concern is with the *forms* of grammatical structures and their relationship to one another, rather than with their meanings or their uses in different contexts. A grammarian interested in this kind of description will often use for analysis sentences that have been made up to illustrate grammatical rules rather than sentences drawn from real world sources.

Another approach sees language first and foremost as a system of communication and analyses grammar to discover how it is organised to allow speakers and writers to make and exchange meanings. Rather than insisting on a clear distinction between grammatical and ungrammatical forms, the focus is usually on the appropriateness of a form for a particular communicative purpose in a particular context. The primary concern is with the *functions* of structures and their constituents and with their meanings in context. A grammarian interested in this kind of description is likely to use data from authentic texts (the term *text* is used here for both spoken and written language) in specific contexts.

The former approach to grammatical analysis is often called **formal**, while the latter approach is normally called **functional**.

c) Write a one-paragraph definition of 'poverty' using only the information in Ex. 6. Text study (ii).

4

I. Cause and Effect

1 Read the following sentences. In each sentence:
- which is the *cause* and which the *result* or *effect*?
- what is the phrase that joins the *cause* to the *effect*?

a Boredom at work can lead to low levels of productivity and high levels of absenteeism.

b Residents believe that, with some assistance, local planning can give rise to an environment completely to their liking.

c The bad performance of large parts of the manufacturing industry was the cause of Britain's relatively poor economic record at that period.

2 Read the following sentences. In each sentence:
- which is the *cause* and which the *result* or *effect*?
- what is the phrase that joins the *cause* to the *effect*?

a The British countryside continued to be affected during the 1970s when more elm trees were cut down owing to Dutch Elm Disease.

b Owing to the larger number of learners and a shortage of teachers in nursing education, medical schools are creating more courses based on learning by discovery, with the teacher acting as guide, counsellor and facilitator.

c The fall in the consumption of fish is partly due to reduced demand and partly to increasing prices, in turn resulting from reduced catches.

d Thailand's efforts to stem serious erosion problems resulting from the extension of cultivated land as a result of population growth and large-scale destruction of forests by logging companies are reported to be largely ineffective (Kilakuldilok 1981).

Now answer these questions about the last group of sentences:
- what is the difference between 'b' and the other sentences?
- what is the difference between 'c' and the other sentences?
- what is the difference between the positions of cause and effect in the sentences in exercise 1 above, and the sentences in exercise 2?

Reading passage

3 Pre-reading
Look at the following words and phrases and discuss their meaning with the rest of your class:

malnutrition   deficiency   adequate diet   undernourished   protein
calories   mental retardation   vital organs.

Use the information in the following text to complete the table on page 30.

(1) Many diseases may **result** if a person does not have an adequate diet. Protein deficiency diseases such as kwashiorkor are particularly damaging; they **lead to** mental retardation, particularly when they occur in young children. Vitamin and mineral deficiencies can **lead to** weak bones, loss of teeth, blindness, or failure of any of a number of vital organs. Children who
5 do not receive sufficient protein or calories develop characteristic bloated bellies, thin arms and legs, wide eyes and shrivelled skin. Perhaps even more sinister is the fact that severe malnutrition in young people **leads to** early and irreversible brain damage. This **results in** a negative feedback cycle, for if undernourished and retarded children survive to become adults, they will be likely to have a hard time finding work and if work is found it is often of the kind that
10 pays the least money. When these impoverished adults in turn have children, their young are likely to be undernourished as well, **thereby** perpetuating the tragic cycle.

(2) Other diseases **caused by** nutritional deficiency are common throughout the world. By one estimate, a quarter of a million children become permanently blind every year **because** their diets are deficient in Vitamin A. Another 200,000 people per year become deaf **owing to** a lack
15 of iodine. An additional uncounted number of individuals die of infectious diseases **because** their bodies and immune systems have been weakened by hunger and lack of proper nutrients. In total, some 15 million people starve to death or die indirectly from malnutrition every year.

Causes	Results
Protein deficiency	mental retardation
Vitamin and mineral deficiency	
	bloated bellies, thin arms and legs, wide eyes and shrivelled skin
Severe malnutrition	
Lack of Vitamin A	
	deafness

4 Language Focus

Look at the reading passage again. Put the words and phrases in bold, which describe cause and effect relationships, under the headings below.

- Add words and phrases to the lists.
- What is the function of the words *may* and *can*? What difference do they make to the meaning of the sentences?

Verb (may be followed by a preposition)	Subordinator (before S + V)	Preposition (before NP)	Adverb + verb + *-ing*

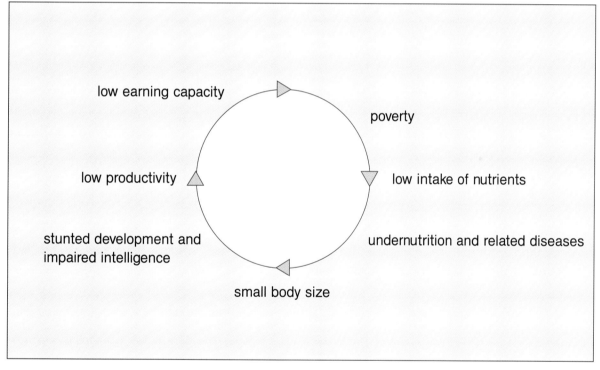

Figure 4.1. A schematic representation of the poverty cycle.

5 **Language for describing causes and effects**

Verbs:

| Lack of protein | (may) cause(s)
(can) lead(s) to
(can) result(s) in
(can) give(s) rise to | mental retardation. |

Reduced relative clauses:

Kwashiorkor is a disease <u>caused by</u> insufficient protein.

Beri-beri is a disease <u>resulting from</u> vitamin deficiency.
Vitamin deficiency can cause metabolic disorders, <u>resulting in</u> mental handicap.

Nouns:

| One | effect
consequence
result | of vitamin A deficiency is blindness. |

The cause of Kwashiorkor is insufficient protein over an extended period.

Prepositions:

| 200,000 people per year become deaf | owing to
because of
as a result of | a lack of iodine. |

Scurvy is a disease which is <u>due to</u> vitamin C deficiency.

'thereby + -ing'

| Their young are likely to be undernourished as well, | thereby
thus | perpetuating the
tragic cycle. |

Subordinators:

An additional number of individuals die of infectious diseases <u>because</u> their bodies and immune systems have been weakened by hunger and lack of proper nutrients.

Connectors:

If undernourished and retarded children do survive to become adults, they have decreased learning ability. | Therefore,
Consequently,
Because of this,
As a result of this, | when they grow up, it may be difficult for them to get work. |

6 **Gap-fill exercise:**
Use the words and phrases from the list to complete the following sentences.

as a result   *because*   *consequently*   *due*   *resulting*   *thereby*

a .... of severe malnutrition, young children may become brain damaged.
b Agricultural improvements .... from drainage enabled both small and large landowners to improve their position.

c The Business School is acutely aware that the world of business is global. ...., many of the courses have units explicitly concerned with Europe and Asia.

d Technical secondary schools in Malawi have shown very large drops in enrolment, mainly .... of unemployment among their graduates .... to a collapse in the productive sectors of the economy.

e The problem of water shortage was compounded by a series of hot summers which increased the rate of soil evaporation, ... reducing further the amount of water which penetrated through to the aquifers.

f In winter, the sun's rays have to travel through more of the Earth's absorbent atmosphere to reach the ground than they do when the sun is overhead, ... in a drop in temperature.

7 **Gap-fill exercise:**
Use the words and phrases to complete the following sentences.

affected by   *as a result*   *caused*   *depends*   *gives rise*   *give rise*

a Improved scientific knowledge generally .... to improved accuracy in forecasting.

b A diet which consistently lacks a sufficient quantity of a particular vitamin is certain in time to .... to the corresponding vitamin deficiency disease.

c Kwashiorkor is one of the conditions .... by protein deficiency.

d The quality and character of coffee beans is .... climate and varying soil types in which they grow.

e The effects of nutrition on health are both direct and indirect as in many ways health .... on the quantity and quality of diet.

f On March 14, the U.S. Health Department published statistics showing that more American teenage males died .... of gunshot wounds than from all natural causes combined.

8 **Discussion: strength and certainty of causal relationships**
Study the sentences in the box below. Rank the sentences according to how strongly they express a cause/effect relationship.

a	The human papilloma virus is linked to most cervical cancer.
b	Stomach cancer in many cases may be associated with certain bacterial infections.
c	Smoking causes most lung cancer.
d	Dyes used in certain industries increase the risk of bladder cancer.

II. Problems and Solutions

Formal academic texts sometimes have the following format:

Situation or **Background**: Who is involved, when and where is this happening; what is the situation and context of the 'problem' that follows.

Problem: What difficulty/need/complication/doubt has emerged out of the 'situation'?

Solution: How is/was the 'problem' resolved, or overcome?

Evaluation: How good was the solution? If there is more than one solution, which is the best?

9 **Reading:**
Read the text on child poverty. It looks at the problems children face in developing countries and some solutions to those problems.

(1)   A recent study concluded that over 1 billion children – more than half the children in developing countries – suffer from at least one form of severe deprivation. The investigation also confirmed that children suffer a range of problems that overlap one another: poor nutrition makes children vulnerable to sickness and diarrhoea, which can then pollute the local water that
5   children use, which then causes weight loss and reduces resistance to disease. Furthermore, children who are poorly fed, frequently ill or live in crowded homes with no electricity are likely to encounter more problems at school. Children experience poverty with their hands, minds and hearts. Thus material poverty, such as starting the day without a nutritious meal, or engaging in hazardous labour, hinders emotional capacity as well as bodily growth.

10   (2)   Poor access to education, food or health-care services also has particular implications for girls and women. There are large differences between the numbers of girls and boys who have never attended school. Providing education for girls leads to greater employment for women. In addition, countries that have higher rates of education among women also have far less child poverty.

15   (3)   Each year, tens of millions of children are victims of exploitation, violence and abuse. The effects of these abuses are far-reaching and enduring. They rob children of their childhood, preventing them from fulfilling anything close to their full potential. Families form the first line of defence for children. The further away children are from their families, the more vulnerable they are to risk. Children separated from their families are more likely to be marginalised, abused and
20   live in poverty in adulthood, and are less likely to develop vital social skills as well as community support and interaction. The countries that have the best records in terms of preventing child poverty offer generous support for families with children. For example, the Oportunidades programme, launched in Mexico in 1997, grants cash transfers on the condition that members of a household are certified as attending school and health clinics. The results have been
25   significant and consistent. In rural areas covered by the scheme, there has been a 57 per cent rise in visits to health clinics and significant reductions in under-five mortality. In Madagascar, one solution has been a comprehensive child survival programme which helps to reduce infant mortality. The programme includes activities to vaccinate every child, to ensure that every mother and newborn is protected by insecticide-treated mosquito nets and to provide free oral
30   rehydration packs.

(4)   Another major problem for children in developing countries is the pressure put on them to work. A recent study by the International Programme on the Elimination of Child Labour offers convincing evidence that, over a 20-year period, the economic benefits of eliminating child labour would far exceed the costs.

35   (5)   Children themselves help us understand what child poverty means. In Serbia and Montenegro, a country impoverished by more than a decade of war and economic crisis, UNICEF has been working on a participatory study of child poverty that has made a point of consulting children in discussions that are set up like games. Consulting children leads to better targeting of education, health and social assistance services towards the poor.

Now re-read the text and complete the following table:

➤ = causes/leads to

Background	Problem (by paragraph)	Solution	Evaluation
I billion children suffer from at least one form of deprivation	**1** Poor (i) .... ➤ sickness & diarrhoea ➤ (ii) .... bad water ➤ (iii) .... Overcrowding/ poor food/illness ➤ (iv)		
	2 Girls do not (i) .... Girls are not (ii)	Greater rates of (iii) .... among women.	**a** Greater women's (iv) .... **b** Reduction of (v) ....
	3 Children victims of (i)	**a** Support for children in (ii)	
		b Mexico: (iii)	(iv) .... and drop in (v) ....
		c Madagascar: (vi)	Drop in (vii) ....
	4 Pressure on children to work	(i)	Economic benefits
	5 Child poverty following war	(i)	Better (ii) ....

Look through the table you have just completed. Now discuss the following questions:
- **What is the relationship between the various 'problems' in paragraph 1?**
- **What is the relationship between the various 'solutions' in paragraph 3?**
- **What do you feel about the various solutions and the evaluations of the solutions that are outlined in this passage?**

10 **Reading**
Read this passage adapted from an academic article on health problems suffered by young doctors and complete the table below. Before doing this, discuss the meanings of the words in bold.

(1) ... it seems that the young doctors suffer from fairly frequent minor illness. The common respiratory infections may well be due to the fact that they are under stress and are also exposed in hospitals to a higher risk of infection. In terms of mental health, there are no direct comparisons but the **prevalence** of psychiatric symptoms is comparable with other research on
5 junior medical staff. Firth-Cozens found 50% of junior doctors with symptoms that required treatment. This was much higher than most community samples; the doctors were in their preregistration year, however, and when sampled again, later in their careers, the rate had dropped to 36%, similar to other health workers (Firth-Cozens, 1995).

(2) The reports of the doctors' own health care have several implications for the health and well-
10 being of doctors and their management. Young doctors are not treating themselves properly when ill: they carry on working, they **self-prescribe** and they ask a friend or colleague to treat them rather than go for a proper independent consultation. This is of particular concern in relation to psychiatric problems where it is generally inappropriate to be treated by a colleague or friend. If such behaviour is clearly apparent at this stage in their careers, it is easy to see how patterns for
15 the future become established. From statistical evidence on the medical profession, we know that in the future, a proportion of these doctors are likely to suffer from depression or alcohol problems and from the evidence presented here, they are unlikely to seek help appropriately.

(3) These doctors are not aware of the Occupational Health Service and are not in the habit of using it. If this service is planned to be for the use of medical staff, consideration should be given
20 nationally to its promotion. If not, alternative services need to be developed. Such services must be well-known, accessible and **confidential**. More importantly, the climate of **stoicism** needs to be altered at an early stage in medical careers. Whether this is a cultural phenomenon first developed at the undergraduate level, or simply due to the pressure of work and lack of cover arrangements in the NHS, the problem has to be addressed as a matter of priority. Failure to do
25 so jeopardises doctors' own health, the welfare of their colleagues and families and patient care.

Paragraph 1:	a) Background Young doctors suffer from fairly frequent minor illnesses.	b) Problems
Paragraph 2:	a) Problems	b) Future Problems (note the language used)
Paragraph 3:	a) Problems	b) Solutions (note the language used)

This 'Background/Situation – Problem – Solution – Evaluation' organisation of academic text structures can be found in paragraphs, chapters and whole books.

11 **Writing Task**
Write a similar text to either Ex. 9 or Ex. 10 about one of the following:
- air pollution
- climate change
- drug abuse
- urbanisation
- unemployment
- educational failure

Your answer should refer to the background, problems and solutions and should give an evaluation of the solutions.

1 **Pre-reading**
- **What does it mean to you, to be able to read and write?**
- **Do you know anyone who cannot read or write? How does this change their life?**
- **What would life be like in a society where people could not read or write?**
- **What disadvantages are there when you <u>can</u> read and write?**

2 **Reading**
Now read the following passage. It describes the differences between societies that have writing and those that do not. Answer the questions in the right hand column.

(1) Supporters of the 'Great Divide' theory agree that something is lost as well as gained when people become literate; but they consider it is worth losing some benefits in order to obtain many others.

(2) Writing can give permanence to the strings of meaning that issue from
5   our mouths. Writing freezes thoughts and ideas and this means that the same sequence of words can be referred to yesterday, today and tomorrow. What was written ten years ago can be compared to what will be written ten years in the future. Therefore, reference becomes possible; reference books, lists and tables become an integral part of life. The total
10   number of words in any written language can far outstrip the total words that any individual can hold in their memory. In typographic cultures, one can always look the words up in a dictionary. Oral languages, in contrast, tend to have vocabularies of only a few thousand words and **these** are *What does 'these'* generally limited to things that can be experienced. *refer to?*

15 **(3)** Writing also alters the way we look at the past. Oral communities tend to accommodate the memory of the past to the reality of the present. **This** *What does 'this'* is not to bend the truth but rather to harmonise the social situation at the *refer to?* time. Literate societies may be constrained by the past, whereas oral societies tend to be anchored in the present and immersed in the here and
20   now. Literate societies have a very definite awareness of time; past, present and future. Clocks, calendars and diaries surround their peoples. Newspapers and television constantly announce the date and the time. The date and time is prominently displayed in banks, post offices and railways stations. By contrast, many people in oral societies, have little idea
25   of the calendar year of their birth. However, they do not feel that they lack anything by not having this knowledge. Their lives are not ruled by the clock but by the sun, the seasons, the hours of daylight and also by their own bodies.

(4) Writing also allows you to communicate over distance; the person you
30   address need not be within sight. This, of course, alters the way the message is conceived. In a face-to-face encounter the words themselves may not be so important, but the way they are said may speak volumes. With writing, however, all of **that** is reduced to some letters and punctuation *What does 'that'* marks on the page. Greater care needs to be taken, therefore, to reduce *refer to?*
35   ambiguity and misunderstanding. Sentences become more complicated with a tendency towards conciseness and precision. Whereas with orality the meaning is in the context and cannot be extricated from it, with writing the meaning is in the language itself.

3 Text analysis

Complete the diagram from the text.

- What is the difference between the paragraph organisation in paragraph 2, and the paragraph organisation in paragraph 3 and the paragraph organisation in paragraph 4?

<u>**Paragraph 2:**</u>

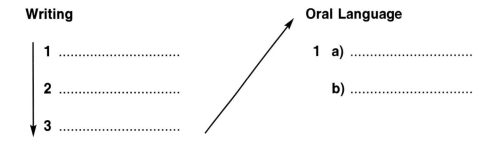

<u>**Paragraph 3:**</u>

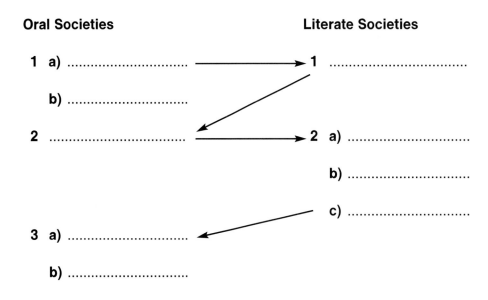

<u>**Paragraph 4:**</u>

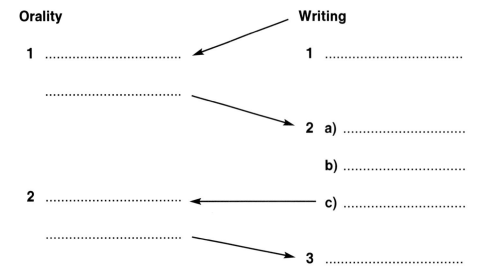

4 Gap-fill exercise
- **Complete the sentences below with one of the following words or phrases:**

  whereas   instead of   in/by contrast   while

- **What do you notice about the punctuation around the words and phrases?**

a In typographic cultures, a language can have a vocabulary of over half a million words. Oral languages, ..., usually have a vocabulary of only a few thousand words.

b On a per capita basis, Mongolia receives the most overseas development assistance, ... Norway donates the most.

c The second aim is to ensure that as many products as possible can be reused or easily repaired .... being thrown away after just one use.

d .... older language learners are often forced to speak, younger learners in an informal second language environment are allowed to be silent until they are ready to speak.

5 Gap-fill exercise
- **Complete the sentences below with one of the following words or phrases:**

  while   however   in contrast to   alternatively

- **What do you notice about the punctuation around the words and phrases?**

a Saudi Arabia, Norway and the Netherlands each give over 1 per cent of their GNP to overseas aid. ...., the United States gives only 0.2 per cent of its GNP to overseas aid.

b .... error correction and explicit teaching of rules are not important to language acquisition, in conscious language learning they are generally thought to be very important.

c .... television, the press is highly differentiated: that is, different papers reach very different audiences with very different messages.

d Should the investigation be conducted from the beginning again or, ..., should it be started as a review of the previous investigation?

6 Language used to compare and contrast

Describing similarities

a. Adjectives
- The mode of processing used by the right brain is similar to *that* used by the left brain.
- The mode of processing used by the right brain is comparable in complexity to *that* used by the left brain.
- The mode of processing of the right brain and *that* of the left brain are similar.

b. Nouns
There are a number of similarities between young children's L1 acquisition and adults' L2 learning.

c. Connectors
Young children learning their first language need simplified, comprehensible input. Similarly, low level adult L2 learners need graded input supplied in most cases by a teacher.

d. Other structures
Both young children's L1 acquisition and adults' L2 learning generally take place in a 'safe environment'.

5

Describing differences

a. Adjectives
- Oral cultures are <u>different from</u> literate cultures in a number of respects.
- Oral cultures are <u>unlike</u> literate cultures with respect to notions of time.

b. Nouns

There are a number of very important <u>differences between</u> literate cultures and oral cultures.

c. Verbs
- Oral cultures <u>differ from</u> literate cultures in a number of important ways.
- Oral cultures and literate cultures <u>differ</u> | with respect to notions of time.
    | as far as notions of time are concerned.

d. Subordinators
- Oral societies tend to be very anchored in the present, <u>whereas</u> literate societies have a very definite awareness of the past.
- <u>While</u> it is very difficult to get away from calendar time in literate societies, many people in oral communities have little idea of the calendar year of their birth.

e. Connectors

It is very difficult to get away from calendar time in literate societies. <u>By contrast</u>, many people in oral communities have little idea of the calendar year of their birth.

f. Prepositions

<u>In contrast to</u> people in literate societies, many people in oral communities have little idea of calendar time.

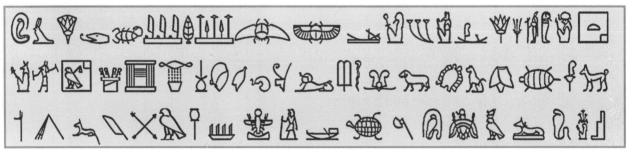

Figure 5.1. Hieroglyphics: an early system of writing mainly in pictorial characters used by the ancient Egyptians

(7) Language study
Study the following transformations, used to achieve a more concise style.

The idea of time in oral cultures is quite different from the idea of time in literate cultures.

➡

The idea of time in oral cultures is quite different from **that** in literate cultures.

Also:

The mode of processing used by the right brain is comparable in complexity to **that** used by the left brain.

After analysis, the opinions of males were found to be different from **those** of females in a number of respects.

Now transform the sentences that follow on the next page in a similar way.

a Food eaten in northern Europe is quite different from food eaten in southern Europe.

b The survey suggests that the situation in Manchester is similar to the situation in Athens.

c The Arabic which is spoken in Morocco is very different from the Arabic which is spoken in Bahrain.

d Programmes on German television are quite similar to programmes on British television in a number of respects.

e The answers given by the students in Group A were not very different from the answers given by the students in Group B.

f The geological composition of the planet Mars is quite different to the geological composition of the planet Earth.

8 Writing exercise

Using words such as *whereas*, *however* **and** *in contrast*, **write sentences comparing:**

- **using a car and using a bicycle.**
- **reading a book and watching a film.**
- **cats and dogs.**
- **Europe and the USA.**
- **writing emails and sending letters by post.**
- **English and your own language.**

9 Writing Tasks

Look at the table below. It summarises in note form some of the main differences between the way a young child learns his/her first language and the way an adult learns a second language.

- **Do you agree with all the points? Why?/Why not?**
- **Would you add anything?**

L1 acquisition in children	L2 learning in adults
language needed for emotional expression and play surrounded by language in natural environment L1 acquired subconsciously	adults need language for a variety of situations little time to learn adults have developed cognitive skills: memorise, make lists, use dictionaries adults read/write often before they speak. adults more self-conscious some/most/all? language learnt consciously and helped by the explicit presentation of rules
simplified, comprehensible input required: supplied first from mother and close family acquisition takes place in known environment – the home	simplified, comprehensible input required: supplied in most cases by teacher and teacher's resources learning/acquisition takes place in safe environment – the classroom.

Now write a number of sentences describing some of the differences and similarities between L1 'acquisition' and L2 'learning'.

5

10 **Text Organisation:**

As you have seen above, compare-contrast texts are often organised in one of two ways:

Pattern 1:
Introductory statement:

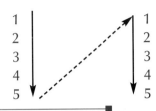

Pattern 2:
Introductory statement:

Now read this text. It compares language acquisition with language learning. Which of the patterns above does this text follow?

(1) Monitor Theory suggests that adults have two Independent systems for developing ability in second languages: the first is subconscious language *acquisition* and the second is conscious language *learning.*

(2) Language *acquisition* is very similar to the process children use in acquiring first and second
5 languages. It needs meaningful interaction in the target language, that is, it needs natural communication. Thus the speakers are not concentrating on the way they are speaking but are focussed on the messages they are giving and receiving. Error correction and explicit teaching of rules are not relevant to language acquisition. However, native speakers can alter their speech to help learners to understand and these changes are thought to help the acquisition process.
10 It has been suggested that there is a fairly stable order of acquisition of structures in language acquisition; one can see clear similarities across learners as to which structures are acquired early and which later. Such learners need not have a conscious knowledge of the rules they have learned, and they may self-correct only because they have a 'feel' for the grammar.

(3) Conscious language *learning*, on the other hand, is thought to be helped by a good deal of
15 error correction and the presentation of rules. When the teacher corrects errors, it is suggested, he or she helps the learner to gain a correct mental 'picture' of the rule. However, whether such feedback has this effect to a large degree remains open to question. No one has claimed that there is only one order for learning a language, although syllabuses usually run from the simple to the complex, while this might not be the same as the sequence in which native speakers
20 acquire their language.

Now write a short summary of the above passage (60 words).

11 **Writing Task**
Write a short text comparing certain aspects of your country with those of the United Kingdom. You might consider writing about some of the following areas: geography, economy, culture and customs, language. Organise your writing in one of the ways indicated in Ex. 10 above.

1 Pre-reading
- **Why do academic writers write about the past? Where in their texts do they do this?**
- **What is academic freedom? What is university autonomy? Why are these things important?**
- **Can you explain what the following terms mean:** *'a tenured professor', 'a leftist professor', 'politically dissident'*?

2 Reading
Read the text below, and make a summary of the main ideas in each paragraph.

(1) Academic freedom has a long and controversial history. For centuries, church and civil authorities placed restrictions on the academic community in terms of teaching, research, and public expression. The Catholic Church forbade the teaching of theological and scientific doctrines in the universities that were contrary to accepted doctrines. Martin Luther, a professor
5 of theology, found himself in conflict with the church officials because of his theological views and was removed from his professorship. It was only later, when some German universities in areas that had turned Protestant became sympathetic to his views, that he was able to resume his academic duties. As the result of many struggles, and especially following the rise of the research university in the 19th century, freedom of expression gradually expanded, and
10 professors were given more latitude in their teaching and research.

(2) Academic freedom has always been a contested terrain, even in academic systems with strong historical traditions. Academic freedom was effectively obliterated in Nazi Germany despite the fact that its modern ideal was a German invention. Not only were direct restrictions placed on what could be taught in German universities during the Third Reich, but tenured
15 professors who did not conform to the new ideology as well as professors who were Jewish or known to be politically dissident were fired. Few voices were raised in protest in Germany against these developments, and both the German professors' organisations and the students' unions supported the Nazi suppression of academic freedom. In many cases, the universities themselves implemented the changes.

20 (3) During the Cold War anticommunist hysteria in the United States, academic freedom was challenged by governmental authorities seeking to rid the universities of alleged Communists. In some cases such as in public universities in California and New York, a number of professors were forced from their positions by state regulations. In others, investigations "exposed" leftist professors, leading to firing and forced resignations. Some universities protected their
25 professors in the name of academic freedom, while others gave in to outside pressure and fired professors. While only a few faculty were actually fired during this period, academic freedom was imperilled in an atmosphere of repression and many academics feared dismissal. These examples show that even in countries with strong academic traditions and commitments to academic freedom, universities can suffer serious consequences.

30 (4) The Latin American academic tradition also contributed to an important concept in the debate about academic freedom. The idea of university autonomy enshrined in the Cordoba reforms of 1819 has long been a powerful force in Latin America (Walter, 1968). What originated as a student protest resulted in significant reform of the universities not only for Argentina, but also for most of Latin America. Many of the continent's universities are by law and tradition
35 autonomous. This has implications for relations with the state as well as for academic freedom. The autonomous ideal provided significant protection for the professors and students during periods of political unrest in Latin America. The protection has not been complete, especially during the era of military dictatorships during the 1960s and 1970s, but has nonetheless been a central part of the continent's thinking about higher education.

3 Intensive reading
Are these statements true (T) or false (F) according to the text?

a	Martin Luther was a professor of theology who found himself in conflict with the Protestants.	**T/F**
b	Academic freedom was an important ideal in Nazi Germany.	**T/F**
c	Many Nazi professors lost their jobs during the Third Reich.	**T/F**
d	There was very little protest against the Nazi restrictions on academic freedom.	**T/F**
e	In the United States during the Cold War era academic freedom was under threat.	**T/F**
f	For many years university autonomy has been an important tradition in Latin America.	**T/F**

4 Language study
Look at the first two sentences from the second paragraph. What can you say about the forms of the verbs and the time frames they describe?

1 Academic freedom *has always been* a contested terrain, even in academic systems with strong historical traditions.

2 Academic freedom *was effectively obliterated* in Nazi Germany despite the fact that its modern ideal was a German invention.

Figure 6.1. A picture of Martin Luther in 1548.

5 Language for writing about specific times in the past

Adverbial time phrases

For	centuries many years	church authorities placed restrictions on academics.
In the	early 19th century, mid 19th century, late 19th century, 19th century, second half of the 19th century	academic freedom of expression gradually expanded.
At the end of During After	the era of military dictatorships, the situation began to improve. the cold war ... the Nazi period ... the 1960s and 1970s ...	
Between 1933 and 1945, From 1933 to 1945,	restrictions were placed on German academics.	
In	the middle ages Nazi Germany	there was very little academic freedom.
It was only later that Later	he was able to continue his academic work.	

Simple past tense forms

Some universities *protected* their academic staff.

Others *gave in* to outside pressure and fired professors.

Professors *were given* more latitude in their teaching and research.

It was only later that he *was able* to resume his academic studies.

6 Language check
Do you know the simple past forms of the following verbs?

undertake	*fall*	*grow*	*put*	*spread*	*forecast*	*find*
bring	*raise*	*cost*	*begin*	*upset*	*increase*	*rise*

7 **Other uses of the simple past in writing**

Describing a research method

All the work on the computer *was carried out* using Quattro Pro for Windows and ... (passive)

The pilot interviews *were conducted* informally by the trained interviewer ... (passive)

Describing past research activity with the author/researcher as subject *

Agarwal (1990) *analysed* the data from 72 countries and *concluded* that there was a strong correlation between Y and Z.

Harbison (1977) *investigated* the differential impact of X and Y on Z.

Referring to the content of a previous section of text/chapter

In the last chapter, it *was argued* that ... (passive)

In the previous section it *was explained* that ... (passive)

Describing changes in the past

The mean income of the bottom 20 percent of U.S. families *declined* from $10,716 in 1970 to $9,833 in 1990.

In this same period, the mean income of the top 5 percent *rose* from $116,655 to $148,124.

Describing historical developments within a field

A few years later Michaux *attached* pedals to the front wheel of the machine which *became* known as the 'boneshaker'.

Between 1850 and 1855 the obvious step of coupling cranks to the front wheel *was taken*. (passive)

*other verbs commonly used include: examine, find, carry out, conduct, study, survey, interview, demonstrate

8 **Discussion**
Look at the following sentence. What can you say about the verb forms and the time expression? How can you explain this?

> The protection has not been complete, especially during the era of military dictatorships during the 1960s and 1970s, but has nonetheless been a central part of the continent's thinking about higher education.

9 **Other common uses of the present perfect form in writing**

With the following adverbial phrases

Over the *past few* decades, the world has seen the stunning transformation of Hong Kong, Singapore, the Republic of Korea and Taiwan.

Since 1965, these four economies, known collectively as the four 'dragons' or 'tigers of Asia', have quadrupled their share of world production and trade.

Until recently, there has been little interest in Scandinavia in the history of business administration as an academic discipline.

Recently, these questions have been addressed by researchers in many fields. (passive)

In recent years researchers have investigated a variety of approaches to X but ...

Up to now, the research has tended to focus on X rather than on Y.

To date, little evidence has been found associating X with Y. (passive)

So far, three factors have been identified as being potentially important: X, Y and Z. (passive)

Describing recent research activity with focus on the area of enquiry – usually more than one study

There *have been* several investigations into the causes of illiteracy (Smith, 1985; Jones, 1987).

The relationship between a diet high in fats and poor health *has been widely investigated* (Smith, 1985; Jones, 1987; Johnson, 1992).

The new material *has been shown* to enhance cooling properties (Smith, 1985; Jones, 1987; Johnson, 1992).

Invasive plants *have been identified* as major contributing factors for the decline of many North American species.

10 **Language check**
Do you know the past participle forms of the following verbs?

undertake	*fall*	*grow*	*put*	*spread*	*forecast*	*find*
bring	*raise*	*cost*	*begin*	*upset*	*increase*	*rise*

11 **Gap-fill exercise**
Use either the simple past or the present perfect form of the verbs to complete the following sentences:

a So far, there **(be)** .... little research on how these drugs affect fertility.
b In 1999, Smith and Jones **(establish)** .... that erythromycin has two effects in susceptible bacterial cells.
c All of the participants **(be)** .... aged between 18 and 19 at the beginning of the study.

d Since 1987 there **(be)** .... a modest increase in the number of rural doctors in the province.

e Up to now there **(be)** .... very little information in the medical literature on Hispanics and blood pressure reduction.

f It was Nicholas Copernicus (1473-1543) who **(challenge)** .... the geocentrism of Ptolemy with his own heliocentric universe.

g Following this, the samples **(be)** .... placed in a freezer (Revco Freezer/incubator B0D 30A) at −2°C for an additional 3 weeks.

h Al-Battani (c. 850-929) **(make)** .... his astronomical observations at Rakku over a 40-year period.

i Recent clinical investigations **(show)** .... the importance of the renin-angiotensin-aldosterone system in the progression of heart failure.

j Between 1980 and 2001, energy consumption in Latin America **(grow)** .... by 82% overall.

12 **Language study**
Look at the following transformation.

> Restrictions were placed on what could be taught in German universities during the Third Reich, and tenured professors who did not conform to the new ideology were fired.
>
> ↓
>
> ***Not only were restrictions placed*** on what could be taught in German universities during the Third Reich, but tenured professors who did not conform to the new ideology were fired.
>
> **or**
>
> ***Restrictions were not only*** placed on what could be taught in German universities during the Third Reich, but (also) tenured professors who did not conform to the new ideology were fired.

Now see if you can transform the following sentences in a similar way:

a These findings provide new insights, and they add further fuel to the controversies surrounding Heisenberg.

....

b The students conduct the psychoanalysis of at least three patients under the close and extended supervision of experienced psychoanalysts, and they also undergo a personal analysis.

....

c Nanotubes conduct heat better than any other known material, and they are about a hundred times stronger than steel.

....

d In this case, subsequent experiments failed to reproduce the data, and a much more thorough analysis of the 1999 data failed to confirm the events.

....

e The project is aimed at anticipating events in this region, and it is designed to enhance our limited ability to discern and interpret signs of unrest in other volcanic areas.

....

13 **Further study: Text analysis and discussion**
Read the text below. Using the lettered verb forms, complete the table over the page.

(1) Until the fourteenth century those who **(a)** *were born* with defective eyesight and the aged **(b)** *had* no hope of being able to read or carry out any kind of work that demanded good vision, for until then spectacles **(c)** *were unknown.* Although fundamentally very simple, no spectacles could be made before the discovery of a number of techniques. Apart from a basic
5 understanding of optics and the behaviour of lenses, it was essential to be able to produce clear glass and to know how to grind the lenses to the correct curvature.

(2) As early as the tenth century the Arabs **(d)** *had made* a special study of optics and the diseases of the eye, always prevalent among desert dwelling people. Of these Islamic scholars the most outstanding was Ibn al-Haytham who worked in Egypt. In about 1040 he **(e)** *produced*
10 a treatise on optics in which, for the first time, the true function of the cornea (or lens) of the eye **(f)** *was described.* Al-Haytham not only studied the anatomy of the eye but also the path of light as it was affected by mirrors and glass lenses. Strangely, however, al-Haytham never **(g)** *hit upon* the idea of using lenses to correct faulty eyesight.

(3) By the late twelfth century copies of al-Haytham's treatise on optics **(h)** *were widely*
15 *distributed* throughout the libraries of Islam, most importantly in Spain, then under Arab rule. It was here that his works were translated into Latin, the common language of European scholars. Known to Europeans as Alhazan, al-Haytham's treatise formed the basis upon which many scholars worked. In England, for example, Grosseteste at Oxford University and his most brilliant scholar, Bacon, **(i)** *improved upon* al-Haytham's theories.

20 **(4)** At the same time many outstanding Arab scholars **(j)** *were attracted* to the court of Emperor Frederick II in Sicily. Here too, the works of al-Haytham **(k)** *were translated* into Latin. Thus by the middle of the thirteenth century many European scholars **(l)** *had become* familiar with the basic theories of optics and a small number were producing their own experimental optical equipment. The manufacture, however, of a limited number of lenses for this kind of work was a
25 very different matter from the production of large numbers of lenses as would be required for the widespread use of spectacles.

Figure 6.2. Ibn Al-Haytham's method relied on experiment rather than on past authority. Among his original works, only those on optics, astronomy and mathematics survive.

Infinitive form of phrase	Tense used in text	Reasons for use of tense
a to be born	simple past passive	an action or event that took place at a specific time in the past
b to have	simple past	a continuous state or situation in the past
c to be (un)known	simple past passive	a continuous state or situation in the past
d		An action in the past which occurs before another action in the past or before a mentioned time (+ by)
e		
f		
g		
h		
i		
j		
k		
l		

Language focus: inserting a false subject for emphasis
Look at the transformations in the box below.

Here his works were translated into Latin.

↓

It was here **that** his works were translated into Latin.

Skinner explained behaviour in terms of stimulus-response.

↓

It was Skinner **who** explained behaviour in terms of stimulus-response

---

Make similar transformations to the following sentences emphasising the words which are underlined. Other changes may also have to be made.

a Galileo was the first to see the moons of Jupiter.

b Bacon improved upon al-Haytham's theories.

c Multinationals invest in developing countries to take advantage of the lower production costs.

d The greenhouse effect is responsible for the recent changes in global weather patterns.

e The second part of your argument is flawed.

f Jung developed his theory of the collective unconscious through his work with the dreams of his patients.

g The subjects were classified as being "nice" or "nasty" on the basis of their behaviour.

h The overall balance in the diet is important.

i The second example cited in the text provides us with a key to his character.

 Writing Tasks
a) Write a single sentence summary of one of the passages in this unit.

b) Write one or two paragraphs outlining your academic/professional experiences to date.

c) Write a short account of recent development(s) which have taken place over the last 20- 30 years in your field of study or in your country.

1 Pre-reading
- **What does the graph below tell us about how the population of the United Kingdom will change in the future?**
- **What do you think led to the peaks in births in the last century?**

Figure 7.1. Births and deaths in the United Kingdom since 1901

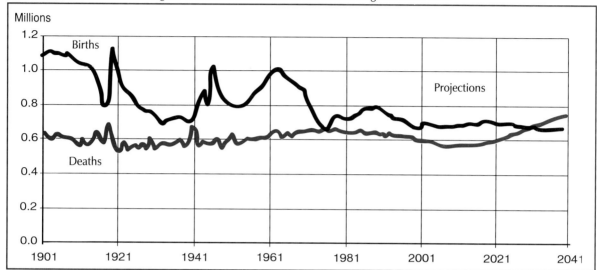

2 Reading
Read the text and decide whether the statements that follow are true (T) or false (F).

(1) Figure 7.1 shows the number of births and deaths in the United Kingdom since 1901. As can be seen, the two world wars had a major impact on births. There was a fall in the numbers of births during the First World War, followed by a post-war 'baby boom', with births peaking at 1.1 million in 1920. The number of births then decreased and remained low during the inter-war years and the Second World

5 War. A second baby boom followed the Second World War, with a further, more sustained increase in fertility and consequent baby boom in the 1960s. In the mid-1970s the number of births fell to similar levels as the number of deaths. There was a mini boom in births in the late 1980s and early 1990s, the result of the larger cohorts of women born in the 1960s, before numbers began falling again.

(2) There were 696,000 live births in the United Kingdom in 2003. This was the largest single

10 year change since 1979 and the highest number of births since 1999, although it is too early to say whether the long-term downward trend in fertility has been reversed. However, births in 2003 were 36 per cent fewer than in 1901 and 23 per cent fewer than in 1971. Projections suggest that the number of births will remain relatively constant over the next 40 or so years, ranging from around 670,000 to 710,000.

15 **(3)** The number of deaths has fluctuated around the 600,000 level for most of the last century with 612,000 deaths registered in 2003. It is projected that the number of deaths will start to increase when the number of people born in the baby boom after the Second World War begin to reach advanced ages. The number of deaths is expected to exceed the number of births from around 2031.

(4) Although the number of deaths each year over the last century remained relatively stable,

20 death rates (per 100,000) fell considerably owing to an increasing population total. Rising standards of living and developments in medical technology and practice help to explain the decline in death rates. Well over half the deaths at the beginning of the twentieth century occurred under age 45. By 2001, 96 per cent of deaths occurred at ages 45 and over. Infant mortality accounted for 25 per cent of deaths in 1901, but had fallen to 4 per cent of deaths by

25 the middle of the last century and to less than 1 per cent in 2003.

a	There were more births in 2003 than in 1971.	**T/F**
b	The number of births peaked during the two world wars.	**T/F**
c	The Second World War was followed by a 'baby boom'.	**T/F**
d	For much of the last century the number of deaths has remained at the 600,000 level.	**T/F**
e	Overall, since 1901 death rates have fallen significantly.	**T/F**
f	By 2001, only 4 per cent of deaths occurred before the age of 45.	**T/F**
g	Accounting for a quarter of all deaths in 1901, infant mortality had fallen to less than 1 per cent of deaths by 2003.	**T/F**

3 **Matching phrases**
Match the phrases on the left with those on the right

a Births in 2003 were 36 per cent	**i** remained low during the inter-war years.
b The number of deaths is expected	**ii** fewer than in 1901.
c There was a fall in the	**iii** will remain relatively constant.
d Infant mortality accounted for	**iv** to exceed the number of births.
e The numbers of births	**v** number of births during WW1.
f Projections suggest that the number of births	**vi** 25 per cent of deaths in 1901.

4 **Sentence reconstruction**
Reconstruct grammatically correct sentences from the following words:

a 696,000 there in 2003 live births were in the United Kingdom
....

b fewer 36 per cent births in 2003 were in 1901 than
....

c births the inter war years during the number of low remained
....

d of deaths accounted 25 per cent infant mortality in 1901 for
....

e developments the decline rates in medicine explain in death help to
....

f had fallen to by the middle deaths of the last century infant mortality 4 per cent of
....

5 Pre-reading
- What does the graph below tell us about the changing pattern of partnerships in the United Kingdom since 1950?
- What do you think has led to these changes?

Figure 7.2. Marriages and divorces in the United Kingdom since 1950

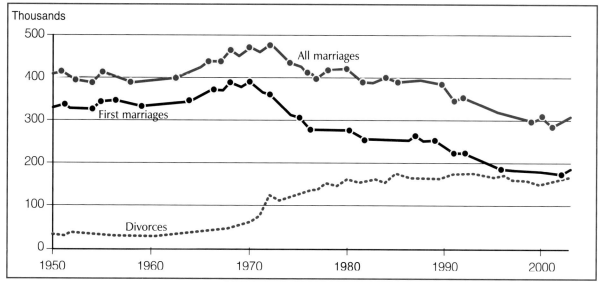

6 Reading
Read the text and decide whether the statements that follow are true (T) or false (F).

(1) The pattern of partnership formation in the United Kingdom has changed since the early 1970s but, despite the decrease in the overall numbers of people marrying, marriage is still the most common form of partnership for men and women. In 2003, around half of the UK population were married. Figure 7.2 shows the number of marriages and divorces in the United

5 Kingdom since 1950. In 1950 there were 408,000 marriages in the United Kingdom. The number grew during the mid- to late-1960s to reach a peak of 480,000 in 1972. This growth was partly a result of the babies born in the post-war boom reaching marriageable ages and, at that time, people were marrying younger than in more recent years. The annual number of marriages then began to decline. However, there was a slight rise in 2003 when the number of marriages stood

10 at just over 306,000.

(2) The number of divorces taking place each year in Great Britain more than doubled between 1958 and 1969. After 1969 divorce was also permitted in Northern Ireland. By 1972 the number of divorces in the United Kingdom had doubled again. This latter increase was partly a 'one-off' effect of the Divorce Reform Act 1969 in England and Wales, which came into effect in 1971.

15 The Act introduced a single ground for divorce which made the process less complicated. Although there was a slight drop in the number of divorces in 1973, the number rose again in 1974 and peaked in 1993 at 180,000. The number of divorces then fell to 155,000 in 2000. In 2003 the number of divorces increased by 4 per cent to 167,000, from 161,000 in 2002. This was the third successive annual rise.

20 **(3)** Following divorce, people often form new relationships and may remarry. Remarriages, for one or both partners, increased by a third between 1971 and 1972 after the introduction of the Divorce Reform Act 1969, and peaked at 141,000 in 1988. In 2003 there were just over 123,000 remarriages, accounting for two fifths of all marriages.

a	The number of marriages in the UK peaked in the early 1970s.	**T/F**
b	Since 1972 the annual number of marriages has steadily declined.	**T/F**
c	There were more than twice as many divorces in 1969 as in 1958.	**T/F**
d	The number of divorces has declined since 1973.	**T/F**
e	Second and subsequent marriages accounted for 40 per cent of all marriages in 2003.	**T/F**

7 **Matching phrases**
Match the phrases on the left with those on the right.

a In 2003 about 50%	**i** peaked at 480,000 in 1972.
b Figure 7.2 demonstrates the	**ii** of people in the UK were married.
c The number of marriages	**iii** to 155,000 in 2000.
d This growth was partially attributed to	**iv** the babies born in the post-war boom reaching marriageable ages.
e The divorce rate then fell	**v** about 30% from 1971 to 1972.
f Second and subsequent marriages went up by	**vi** number of marriages and divorces in the United Kingdom since 1950.

8 **Paragraph reconstruction**
Rearrange the sentences on page 57 to form one coherent paragraph based on the information in Figure 7.3.

Figure 7.3. Live births outside marriage in the UK since 1901

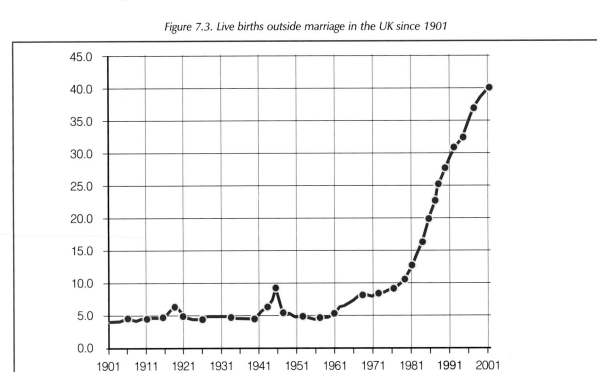

a		As a result, the proportion of live births that occurred outside marriage in the United Kingdom was almost five times greater in 1999 than in 1971.
b		Much of this growth can be accounted for by the increase in births to cohabiting couples; that is parents living at the same address.
c		Figure 7.3 shows that with the exception of the periods immediately after the two world wars, few births occurred outside marriage during the first 60 years of the 20th century.
d		During the 1960s and 1970s, however, this proportion rose and growth became more rapid from the late 1970s onwards.
e		In the United Kingdom, most children are born to married couples but, an increasing proportion of births occur outside marriage.

9 **Language focus**

The texts in this unit contain a wide range of expressions used for describing graphic data, and also draw on some of the other language functions examined in earlier units. Look at the texts again and underline a section of the text which:

a)   describes a trend;

b)   describes a percentage;

c)   describes a ratio or fraction;

d)   compares two sets of numbers/dates.

10 **Language for describing graphs and trends**

Introducing data

Figure 1 | shows ...
| uses information from ... to show ...

As | shown in Figure 1, ...
| can be seen in Figure 1, ...

It can be seen in Chart 12.1 that ...

Describing trends

There has been a ... Figure 12.1 shows a ...	slight gradual steady marked steep sharp	rise increase decrease decline fall drop	in the number of ... in the amount of ... in the rate of ... in the level of ...

The number of first marriages fell by nearly two fifths between 1961 and 1993.
Natural gas consumption rose by 41 per cent between 1971 and 2003.

The proportion of live births outside marriage has increased dramatically since the early 1960s.
North Sea fish stocks have declined steadily since the early 1980s.

Describing high and low points

The number of live births outside marriage reached a peak during the Second World War.

The peak age for committing a crime is 18.

Oil production peaked in 1985.

Gas production reached a (new) low in 1990.

Projecting trends

The number of The level of	Xs X	is projected to is expected to is likely to	decline steadily drop sharply level off	after 2010.

It is	projected anticipated	that the rate of growth will begin to decline.

Projections suggest that the number of births will remain relatively constant over the next 40 or so years.

Highlighting superlatives

In 1993	the United Kingdom Italy	had the	highest lowest	divorce rate in the EU.

In the 2001 International Reading Literacy Study, boys in England had the third highest score (541) and girls had the second highest score (564).

Describing percentages and fractions

The proportion of live births outside marriage reached one in ten in 1945.

In 1960 just over 5% of live births were outside marriage.

East Anglia had the lowest proportion of lone parents at only 14 per cent.

Since 1981, England has experienced an 89% increase in crime.

The number of first marriages in the United Kingdom fell by nearly two-fifths.

In 2004, the proportion of boys reaching the required standard for reading was lower than that of girls.

11 **Describing lines on graphs**
Use the following words and phrases to describe what happened to ferralite production from 1945 to 2000 as shown in the graph below.
eg. *It remained level between 1980 and 1985.*

remain level   low point   rise dramatically
steady increase   peak   fell sharply

Figure 7.4. Global ferralite production 1945 – 2000 (millions of tonnes)

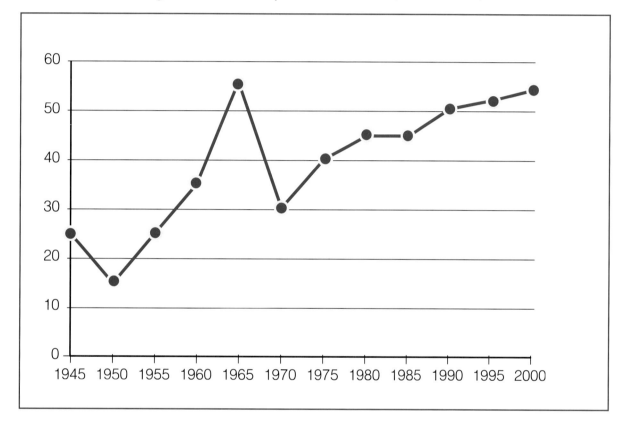

Now make sentences describing production for the following dates and periods.

a 1950

....

b 1960 – 1965

....

c 1965

....

d 1965 - 1970

....

e 1980 - 1985

....

f 1990 - 2000

....

12 **Reading**
Label the lines in Figure 7.5 according to the information in the accompanying text.

Figure 7.5. Consumption of fuels[1] for energy use in the United Kingdom

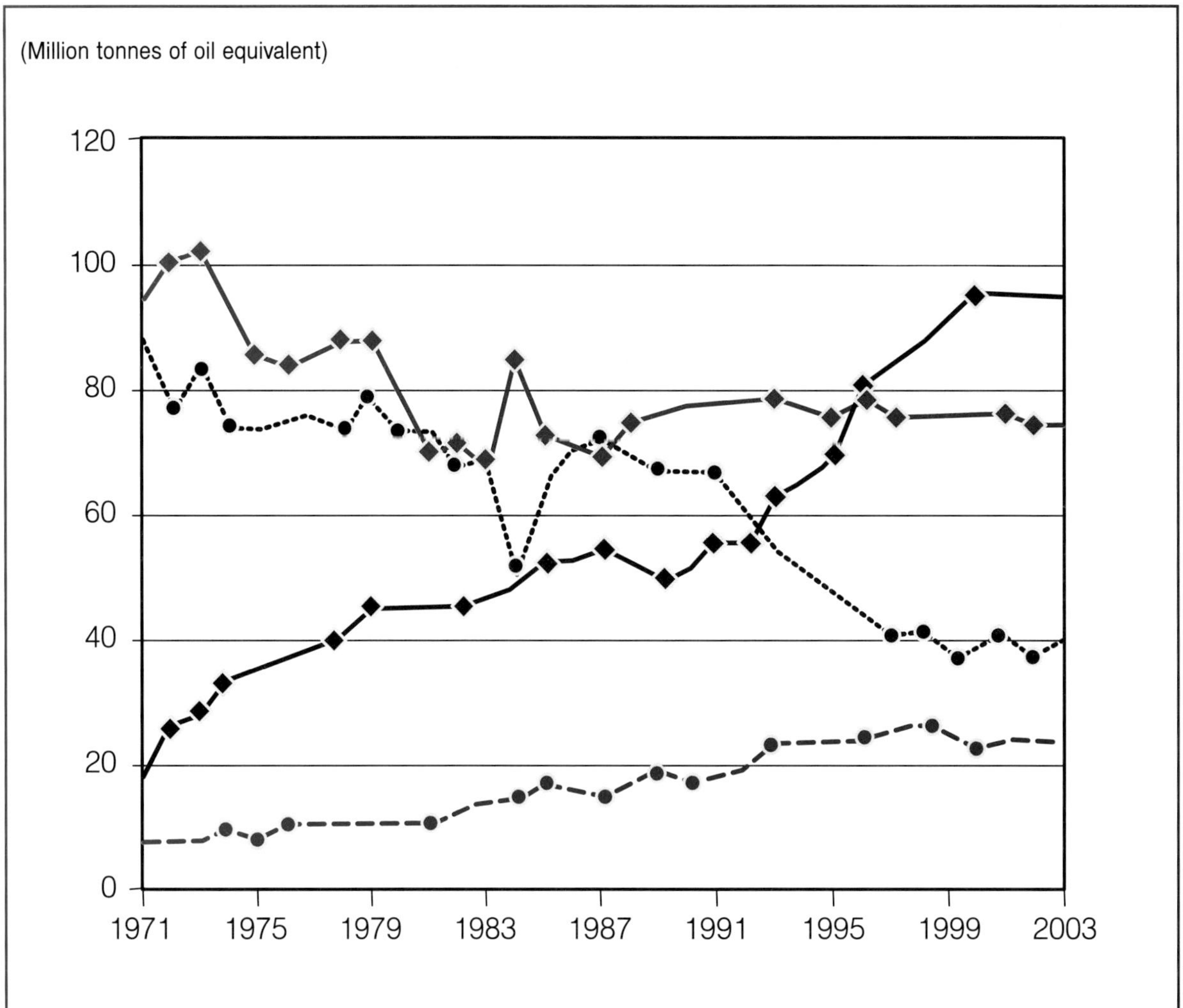

(Million tonnes of oil equivalent)

[1]Includes nuclear, hydroelectric and renewable energy.

Fossil fuels accounted for 90 per cent of fuels used in the production of energy in the United Kingdom in 2003. The use of coal and petroleum for the production of energy fell between 1971 and 2003, by 54 per cent and 21 per cent respectively. However, consumption of petroleum has remained relatively stable since 1990 (Figure 7.5). As total consumption of fuels for energy use
5 has increased by around one fifth since 1983, natural gas and primary electricity production from nuclear energy, hydroelectric and other renewables have become increasingly important. Natural gas consumption rose by 419 per cent between 1971 and 2003. However, between 2000 and 2003, total consumption of all sources of energy has remained steady overall. Renewable electricity can be generated from wind (both offshore and onshore), water (hydro, wave and tidal
10 power), sunlight (the direct conversion of solar radiation into electricity, called photovoltaics or PV), biomass (energy from forestry, crops or biodegradable waste) and from the earth's heat (geothermal energy). None of these forms of generation, except biomass, involves the production of carbon dioxide, and biomass generation produces only the carbon that the material has absorbed from the atmosphere while growing.

13 **Gap-fill exercise**

Complete the text below, which accompanies Figure 7.1, using the correct words from the list.

since   deaths   fall   fairly   peaked   shows   projected   start   decreased

Figure 7.1. **1)** .... the total number of births and deaths in the United Kingdom **2)** .... 1901. The two world wars had a major impact on the number of births in the United Kingdom. There was a noticeable **3)** .... in births during the First World War, followed by a post-war baby boom when the number of births **4)** .... at more than 1.1 million in 1920 – the highest number in any year of the 20th century. The number of births then **5)** .... and remained low during the 1930s Depression and the Second World War. This was followed by a baby boom immediately after the Second World War and another in the 1960s.

The number of births is projected to remain **6)** .... constant over the next 40 years. However, deaths are **7)** .... to start increasing in the 2020s when the larger numbers of people born after the Second World War start to reach advanced ages. If the long term assumption holds that the same number of people leave as enter, then the population of the United Kingdom will **8)** .... to fall once the number of **9)** .... exceeds the number of births from the year 2028.

14 **Matching exercise**

Study Figure 7.6. Then match the phrases on the left with those on the right on page 62.

Figure 7.6. North Sea fish stocks since 1963

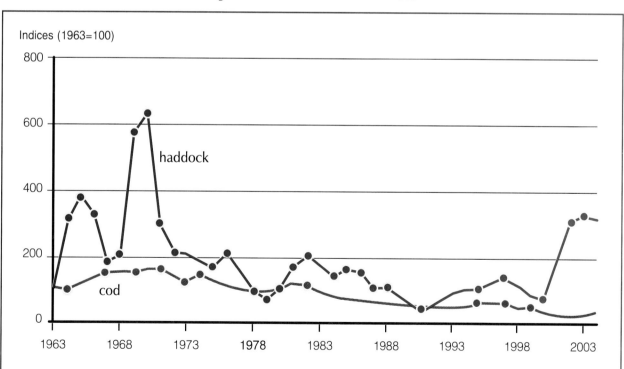

a Fish have traditionally formed an important food resource for many people in the United Kingdom	**i** declined steadily since the early 1980s, and in 2004 were 68 per cent lower than in 1983.
b Figure 7.6 shows	**ii** to the Government and other interested parties.
c Haddock stocks have fluctuated dramatically since the 1960s, and	**iii** on cod fishing during the key spring spawning periods, cuts in the numbers that can be caught and a limit to the number of days each month fishermen can spend at sea catching cod.
d However, stocks of cod in the North Sea and elsewhere are causing particular concern	**iv** the changes in North Sea haddock and cod stocks since 1963.
e After increasing in the 1960s, and fluctuating somewhat in the 1970s, North Sea stocks have	**v** continue to do so: they more than quadrupled between 2000 and 2004.
f The depletion in numbers is thought to have occurred through a combination of	**vi** place that aim to halt and ultimately reverse the decline in cod stocks.
g Measures have been put in	**vii** and they are vital elements of ocean ecosystems.
h These have included restrictions	**viii** overfishing, small numbers of fish surviving to a size where they are taken commercially and possible environmental factors.

Figure 7.7. Haddock is one of the most important food fishes in North West Europe.

15 Text Study

What is the function of the following sentence?

> The depletion in numbers *is thought to have occurred through* a combination of ...

Now look through earlier sections of this unit and find sentences which have an explanatory purpose.

16 **Writing Task**
Write about 150 words on the data in Figure 7.8. Give reasons for the changing trends.

Figure 7.8. Passenger transport: by mode in Great Britain

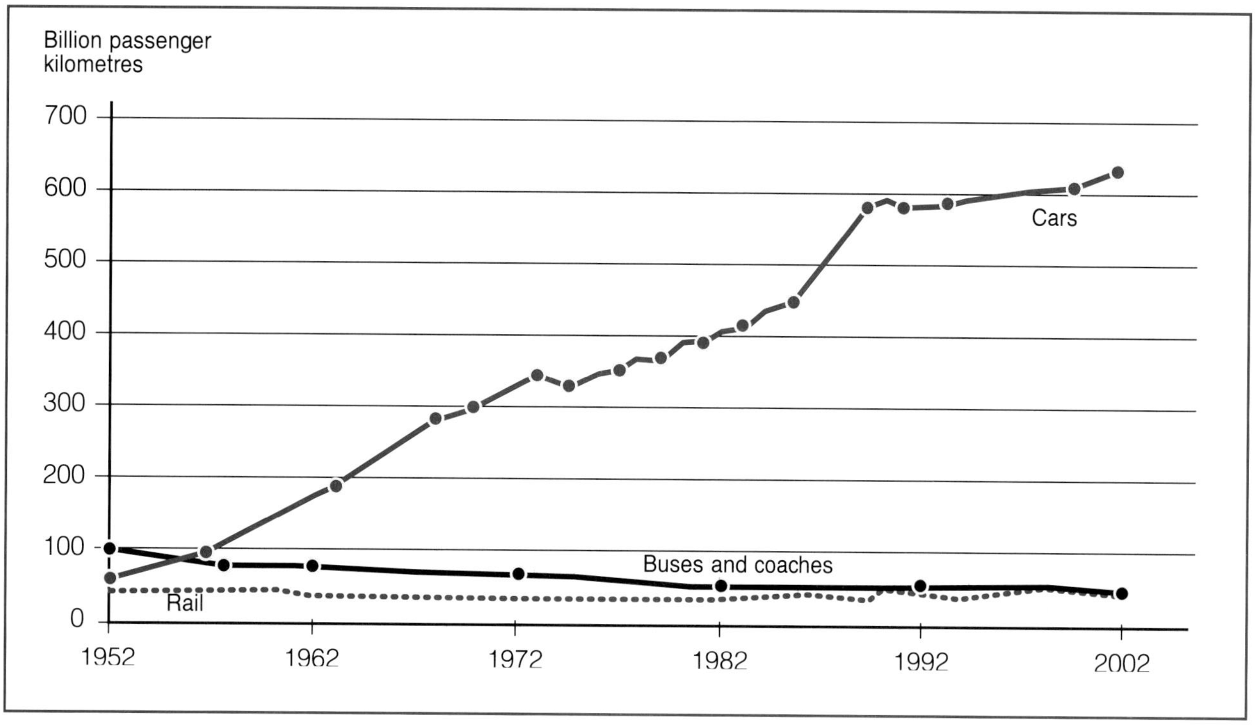

1 **Introductions: Common elements**

There are many ways to introduce an academic essay or assignment. Most academic writers, however, appear to do one or more of the following in their introductions:

- introduce the topic and establish its context and importance
- indicate a problem or controversy, or a knowledge gap in the field of study
- define the topic
- state the purpose of the paper
- provide an overview of the coverage and/or structure of the writing

2 **Text studies**

a) In longer assignments an introduction may require two or three paragraphs, as with the example below. Which of the elements listed at the top of the page can be identified in this introduction?

(1) Higher education is increasingly international, and foreign students are among the most important and visible elements in internationalisation. There are over two million students studying outside the borders of their countries - about a million of these are in OECD nations. The large majority of the world's foreign students are from the developing countries of the Third
5 World but flow patterns are complex and subject to change (Zikopoulos, 1989). Other elements of the internationalisation of higher education are also of considerable importance - the domination of the world's research enterprise by a small number of major industrialised nations, the centralisation of publication and data transmission networks, and the widespread use of English as the world's major scientific language have implications for foreign study as well
10 (Altbach, 1987). In fact, foreign students are at the centre of a complex network of international academic relationships. They are the common embodiments of a worldwide trend toward the internationalisation of knowledge and research in an integrated world economy.

(2) This essay is concerned with several important aspects of the foreign student phenomenon; those relating to the flow of students from the Third World to the industrialised nations including
15 the impact of foreign students on academic institutions and the impact of foreign study on the students as well as the policies relating to these key questions. Its purpose is to reflect on some of the most important generalisations of the available research literature.

b) In shorter pieces of work introductions need not be so well developed. An introduction may be written much more concisely, but still be effective, as with the next example below:

At present, about 2 million students worldwide study outside their home countries, a number which is surely set to increase in the future (Altbach, 2004). Those who study abroad may benefit academically, economically and psychologically from the
5 experience. At the same time, at least in the short term, students studying in countries other than their own may face particular hardships and disadvantages. This short essay will discuss the benefits and some of the 'costs' of overseas study.

Figure 8.1. International students at Manchester University.

Which of the five elements listed in Ex. 1 can you identify in this introduction? What can you say about the order of these elements?

3 Reordering exercises

Reorder the sentences below to form logically sequenced introductions.

Introduction 1

a		Hence the team plays a central role in the development and improvement of any organisation. Everard and Morris even describe it as a 'building block'.
b		This paper will attempt to illustrate the significance of combining the efforts and imaginations of team members and putting them to work in ways which achieve the general as well as specific objectives of an organisation most effectively.
c		The first part of this paper presents a definition of teamwork, and this is followed by a discussion of the characteristics and attributes that a team must have in order to be effective. Team roles as described by Belbin (1987) will also be tackled here.
d		The success of any organisation be it educational, industrial or commercial may depend, among other things, on the ability of all its members to work collaboratively and effectively as a team.
e		It will then move on to examine in some detail the major tasks and roles of the manager as a team leader.

Introduction 2

a		This increase means that there are also an increasing number of wheelchair users. As a result, a large number of houses are having to be adapted, or are purpose built, for wheelchair users.
b		Although both countries tend to face similar problems, the solutions to these problems are not the same in each country.
c		This essay will begin by examining the external modifications to houses for wheelchair users, and then go on to describe the internal features. At the same time it will compare Japanese and British designs, suggesting reasons why these differences occur.
d		Since 1980, the percentage of people over 65 has risen sharply in Japan. According to officials of the Japanese Ministry of Health and Welfare, they will constitute around 20% of the total population by the end of the century.
e		Britain has already adapted a large number of houses for wheelchair use, and this has attracted the attention of designers and architects from Japan.

Introduction 3

a		In most cases, secondary data and personal experience have been used as the sources of information for this paper.
b		In Bangladesh a good number of National and International NGOs have been working in rural and urban areas with different kinds of development programmes.
c		Non-Governmental Organisations (NGOs) have proved their effectiveness in promoting development in many of the world's poorer countries.
d		In this study a brief overview of the activities of NGOs in Bangladesh has been attempted. The scope of the study has been confined to the major areas of their activity.
e		Basically, NGOs initiate development efforts based on micro-social relations at the local level, relying heavily on mutual understanding.

Figure 8.2. Map of Bangladesh and surrounding areas.

4 **Language used in essay introductions**

Introducing the topic (importance, generalisation)

In recent years Recently,	there has been	an increasing interest in ... growing concern about ...

The past decade has seen the rapid development of ...

One of the most important events of the 1970s was ...

There are many situations where ...

X is the leading cause of death in western industrialised countries.

Highlighting a problem in the field or a gap in the literature

However, these rapid changes are having a serious effect ...

The issue of X has been a controversial and much disputed subject within the field of ...

So far, however, there has been little discussion about ...

However, far too little attention has been paid to ...

Focus and aim

This	paper essay	will	focus on ... consider ... review ... critically examine ... survey the trends ...

The aim	of this paper is to ...

This paper will review the research conducted on ... during the period from ... to ...

Outline of structure

The essay has been organised in the following way.

This paper begins by ... It will then go on to ...

The first section of this paper will examine ...

Finally, ...

The paper concludes by ...

Defining and explaining key terms

While a variety of definitions of the term ... have been suggested, this paper will use the definition first suggested by ... who saw it as ...

| Throughout this paper the term ... | will refer to ...
will be used to refer to ...
is assumed to mean ... |

In this article the acronym/abbreviation XYZ will be used.

5 Transformation Exercises
Rewrite the sentences below using the prompts given.

a Recent years have seen a growing interest in the use of laser cutting technology for manufacturing processes.
Rewrite using: *Laser cutting technology ... attracted*

....

b However, these rapid changes are having a serious effect on the global environment.
Rewrite using: *As a result of ... however ... seriously damaged.*

....

c To date, however, no studies have investigated the use of modal verbs for this purpose in any detailed way.
Rewrite using: *So far, however, ... received ... serious attention.*

....

d This short essay will discuss the benefits and some of the 'costs' of overseas study.
Rewrite using: *The purpose ... consider ...*

....

6 Text studies

You are not expected to write the kinds of introductions seen in the extracts above in exams. A much more concise introduction which responds directly to the question is normally sufficient. It may consist of no more than one or two sentences. For example:

The four main reasons for the dissatisfaction with development programmes are: A, B, C and D.

The emphasis and order a writer gives to different elements of an introduction may vary. Study the introduction below and compare its structure with that of the introductions in Exercise 3.

The aim of this essay is to convey to the reader the importance of investment in human capital. It is assumed that the major factor influencing the level of human capital is the degree of investment in education and training. By referring to a simple model of human capital, it is possible to assess the costs and benefits of such investment. The following discussion will
5   distinguish between the social rate of return and the private rate of return, and will also take into account the diminishing marginal rate of return of investment in human capital and capital market imperfections. The distinction between general and specific training and the subsequent consequences to the workers and firm will also be drawn. Finally, a brief reference will be made to other factors that may influence the level of human capital.

7 **Gap-fill exercise**

Fill in the spaces in the introduction below using the following words:

concern   *data*   *consists of*   *important*   *purpose*   *followed*

Modal verbs are used to express ideas such as possibility, certainty, obligation and necessity. *May, might, can, could, will, would, shall, should, ought to* and *need* are some examples. Many studies have demonstrated that the use of modal verbs is an **1)** .... feature of academic writing (Butler, 1982, 1988; Coates and Leech, 1977; Perkins, 1983; Hyland, 1992). Areas of
5   academic texts where modal verbs are found in high frequency are the discussion and concluding sections of research reports and dissertations. It is in these sections that writers assess the evidence presented and carefully draw conclusions from their **2)** .... To date, however, no studies have investigated the use of modal verbs for this purpose in any detailed way. The **3)** .... of the present paper is to examine how modal verbs are
10 used to present evidence in research articles and how they are used to draw conclusions from this. A more specific **4)** .... is how the quality of the evidence and the disciplinary context affect the use and choice of modal verb. The first part of this paper **5)** .... a brief review of the current literature dealing with the use of modal verbs in academic writing. This is **6)** .... by an examination of the use of modal verbs in the results and discussion
15 sections of a small corpus of research articles in the bioscience and in the social science disciplines.

8 **Conclusions: Common elements**

A conclusion is the last section of a piece of writing. It may also be a final decision or judgement. In an academic essay or assignment, the conclusion normally draws together and restates the main points and if appropriate, adds a final comment or judgement. This may sometimes be followed by recommendations. The most common elements are listed below:

Brief restatement of main points
Final comment
     and/or
Judgement/Evaluation
     and/or
Future prospects
     and/or
Recommendation(s)

9 **Text study**
A conclusion may consist of no more than one paragraph, as in the example below.

This short essay has considered some of the main benefits and costs for those students who take the brave step of leaving their home country to study in an educational institution thousands of miles away, where different cultural norms prevail and where a different language may be spoken. The financial costs of studying abroad are usually very high and individuals may
5 experience personal and emotional difficulties. In spite of this, increasing numbers of students are finding that the long term career benefits together with opportunities to acquire new knowledge and experiences, and to gain proficiency in a second language, make the experience worthwhile.

What can we learn about the content of the essay from this conclusion?

10 **Text study**
a) **A good conclusion should give the reader a reasonable idea of the content and structure of the text that preceded it. Does the conclusion below fulfil this requirement?**

b) **After deciding on the function of each sentence in the conclusion, try to identify any phrases or grammatical structures which might be found in other conclusions.**

(1) This paper has given an account of and the reasons for the widespread use of the English language in today's world. Resistance to the use of English and inherent problems with the language itself were also examined, along with some of its more advantageous features. Finally, proposals to make the language easier to learn and more internationally standardised were
5 discussed.

(2) At present there are few other contenders for the status of an international lingua franca. Many other widely spoken languages have strengths, but few match the lexical hybridisation or the inflectional simplicity which give English such wide appeal. Furthermore, no other language has such a dominant role in commercial, diplomatic, scientific and technical fields as English
10 does at the present time. It seems, then, that English, despite its weaknesses and some opposition, will most probably continue to develop as the international language of communication, ideally in a simplified and more standardised form, in the foreseeable future.

11 **Writing Task**
Write an introduction and a conclusion for an assignment that you are currently working on. Pay particular attention to the structure and language of your introductory and concluding sections in the light of the information presented in this unit.

8

12 Dissertations and theses

Introductions and conclusions in dissertations and theses tend to be more fully developed than those we have just analysed. For example, in a study of M.Ed. dissertations at the University of Manchester, the authors found that the average length of the introductions was 635 words, with a range of between 451 - 1386 words. In addition, where the dissertation reports on an original investigation, the following elements are usually included:

Introductions	Conclusions
• research questions or hypotheses to be tested • synopsis of methods • significance of research	• limitations of the study • suggestions for further research

An examination of the dissertations in your departmental library will give you a good idea of how these sections may be developed. In addition, you should consult your departmental guidelines on writing dissertations for a more complete understanding of what is expected.

13 Matching exercise

The following phrases are taken from introductions of dissertations at the University of Manchester. Match the phrases on the left with their functions on the right.

1	Chapter 2 begins by laying out the theoretical dimensions of the research, and ...	a	giving a brief summary of the literature
2	Recently, researchers have shown an increased interest in ...	b	providing a synopsis of the methods
3	Surveys such as that conducted by Smith (1988) showed that ...	c	highlighting a knowledge gap in the field of study
4	The key research question of this study was thus whether or not ...	d	stating the research question(s)
5	The aim of this research project has therefore been to try and establish what ...	e	providing an outline of the dissertation structure
6	The research to date has tended to focus on X rather than Y.	f	explaining the purpose of the research
7	Qualitative and quantitative research designs were adopted to provide both descriptive, interpretive and empirical data.	g	establishing the importance of the topic

1 Pre-reading
List the main advantages and difficulties of studying abroad.

2 Reading
Read the following essay and complete the notes in the boxes on page 74.

(1) One widely acknowledged advantage of going overseas to study is the opportunity to study a chosen subject specialisation which may not be available in a student's own country. Many developing nations, **for example**, offer very limited opportunities for study at the masters and
5 doctoral levels, and the programmes that do exist often cannot compete internationally. **Furthermore**, a person who gains a postgraduate degree from an institution with an international reputation in their chosen subject may feel that they have acquired a certain amount of prestige and, perhaps more importantly, a competitive advantage in the job market in their home
10 country. Degrees from good universities in English speaking countries quite often do confer an advantage in the job markets in other countries.

(2) The **other** advantages of studying abroad have more to do with the fact that it can be an enriching, stimulating and life-changing experience. Students who study overseas deepen their knowledge and understanding
15 of another culture and lifestyle and acquire firsthand knowledge of a different educational system (Cook and Johnson, 2004). **In addition**, those studying abroad have a chance to gain experience of living independently and to make new friends from all round the world. One recent study has shown that the experience of studying abroad helped students to better
20 understand their own cultural values and biases, and contributed to their developing a 'more sophisticated and more balanced way of looking at the world' (Dwyer and Peters, 2004: np).

The first sentence of this paragraph serves two functions. What are they?

(3) Students studying abroad **also** have an opportunity to develop their skills in a second language. **Indeed**, it is generally accepted that one of the
25 best ways of improving proficiency in a second language is to go and live and study in a country where it is spoken. As Goodwin and Nacht (1988:16) stated in their comprehensive review of education abroad programmes 'the mastery of a modern language has traditionally been perceived as the most direct educational benefit of study abroad'. **In fact**
30 one of the reasons why those with educational experience overseas may be more attractive to employers is because of their facility to use an additional language. This is perhaps the main reason why English speaking countries are so popular as study abroad destinations.

What can you say about the position of 'also' in this sentence?

Why does the writer use 'in fact' here?

(4) On the other hand, studying overseas is not without its costs and its
35 hardships. There is, **for example**, a significant price to pay in financial terms. Tuition fees can be very expensive, especially in the sciences and the high prestige subjects like Law and Business Administration. Overseas fees can range from £4,000 to £17,000 per year depending on the institution, the level and the type of course (UKCOSA, 2003). Even
40 applying for courses in some parts of the world can be very expensive. **For example**, in the USA an application alone can cost well over £50 and that does not include the cost of any entry tests a student may be required to take. Apart from the cost of tuition fees, a prospective student also needs

What can you say about the position of 'for example' in this sentence in line 35?

to plan for the costs of living in the country of study, as well as the cost of
45 travelling to and from that country. Many overseas students may actually
face financial hardship unless their family/government is able to support
them adequately.

(5) Even if a student is able to obtain the necessary funding, there are
other costs of studying abroad. Most overseas students will probably
50 experience homesickness and miss the company of their families and
friends at some point during their time abroad. **In addition**, going abroad
as a student means being suddenly confronted with a completely new
environment, language and set of behaviours which often result in a
negative emotional reaction characterised by uncertainty, confusion and
55 antipathy towards the host culture. **This** reaction, which is a consequence   *Which reaction?*
of the individual's incapability of understanding, controlling and predicting
the behaviour of members of the foreign culture, has come to be known as
'culture shock', a term first coined by Oberg (1960). **Nevertheless**, both of
these states tend to be only temporary aspects of life in a new country and
60 those people who experience culture shock usually, in the long term, gain
by learning more about themselves and their culture, and by becoming
more mature in their outlook towards other cultures (UKCOSA, 2003).

(See Unit 8, Ex. 2b and Ex. 9, for the introduction and the conclusion to this short essay. See page 110 for the references.)

Benefits		
Main point 1:	a)	....
	b)	....
Main point 2:	a)	....
	b)	....
Main point 3:		....

Costs		
Main point 4:		....
Main point 5:	a)	....
	b)	....

3 Cohesive devices

Look closely at the text again and discuss the functions of the words in bold. Use the questions on the right hand side of the text to help you.

What do you notice about the positions of adverbial connectors in the sentences in the text? Can you formulate any rules?

One way that writers try to achieve textual cohesion is by using adverbial connectors. These are words or phrases that fall outside the meaning of a sentence but serve to connect one idea to another idea in a different sentence. Connectors may also be used to join ideas across paragraphs or even longer sections of text.

4 Adverbial connectors 1

Match the adverbial connectors to their pragmatic/functional meanings in the tables below. Some of the connectors may have more than one meaning.

Connecting word or phrase	Pragmatic or functional meaning
a Alternatively,	**i** introduces a second fact that exists together with a previous fact, even if it contradicts this
b As a result,	**ii** introduces an additional/opposing idea or point
c At the same time,	**iii** introduces another possible way of doing/thinking about something
d For example,	**iv** introduces an additional point or fact
e Furthermore,	**v** indicates an illustration for support
f Nevertheless,	**vi** indicates consequence

5 Adverbial connectors 2

Match the adverbial connectors to their pragmatic/functional meanings in the tables below. Some of the connectors may have more than one meaning.

Connecting word or phrase	Pragmatic or functional meaning
a However,	**i** introduces a statement which supports or gives more detail about the previous point
b In addition,	**ii** introduces an opposing or alternative idea or point
c In contrast,	**iii** introduces a problem
d In fact,	**iv** introduces a contrasting aspect or fact
e On the other hand,	**v** introduces an effect of something
f Consequently,	**vi** introduces another point or fact

6 **Gap-fill**
Now fill the gaps in the sentences below with an appropriate connecting word or phrase.

alternatively   nevertheless   in fact   consequently   for example   in contrast

a Many companies value the study abroad experience. ...., anecdotal evidence from students who have studied abroad suggests that it is this experience which makes them stand out and sets them on the path to new and attractive opportunities.

b English speaking countries such as the USA, Britain, Australia, New Zealand and Ireland are frequent choices for studying abroad; ...., many students choose to go elsewhere because they are interested in learning a new language.

c In the 2002–03 academic year 584,000 international students were studying at U.S. universities. ...., only one percent of American students, about 161,000, study abroad and a full two-thirds of that one percent head to Western Europe.

d Although some US students go abroad to discover more about a culture that is not their own, some do the exact opposite. ...., students from Arabic-speaking families may study in the Middle East, and Hispanic students may select any of the countries where Spanish is spoken.

e Women might not have the same status or role in the host country that they enjoy at home. ...., they may experience anxiety, confusion, fear, powerlessness or anger.

f Your courses may consist only of formal lectures and a final exam. ...., they may consist of seminars or discussion groups with the expectation that you will complete all of the readings on your own before the final exam.

7 **Language study**
Now look at the two groups of words and phrases in the boxes below and decide how they differ in terms of the sentence structure that follows.

however, in addition, at the same time,	in spite of, with regard to, in the light of,
consequently, on the contrary, as a result	as a result of, because of, in terms of

8 **Matching exercise**
Match the following compound prepositions on the left with their functions on the right.

a on account of	**i** indicates that something exists or happens as an alternative to something else
b in terms of	**ii** specifies an aspect of something you are discussing
c according to	**iii** introduces the reason or explanation for something
d instead of	**iv** indicates a source of information or the source of an idea

9 **Gap-fill exercise**

Now fill the gaps below with one of the compound prepositions from Ex. 8.

a .... style, the paintings Goya produced during this period must count among his best.

b .... killing the cell they inhabit, plasmids often help the host cell by conferring resistance to drugs.

c .... the unexpected number of students, there were insufficient handouts.

d .... the general theory of relativity, space-time is smooth and does not contain any irregular points.

10 **Matching exercise**

Match the following compound prepositions on the left with their functions on the right.

a with regard to	**i**	to introduce information or a fact which results in a decision being made.
b in addition to	**ii**	to introduce a fact which is surprising or which goes against a previous fact
c in spite of	**iii**	to focus attention on the subject of what is being discussed
d in the light of	**iv**	to introduce another item connected with the subject that you are discussing

11 **Gap-fill exercise**

Now fill the gaps below with one of the compound prepositions above.

a .... the overwhelming scientific evidence, many people still refuse to believe that smoking causes lung cancer.

b .... the recent survey data, the government are introducing measures to restrict the number of cars in cities.

c However, the author raises a number of difficulties .... the third point.

d .... homesickness, students who study in other countries may experience culture shock.

12 **Writing tasks**

Now write a short discussion essay on one of the following topics:

i **Why do you think vegetarianism has become so popular?**
Discuss the reasons for and against vegetarianism.

ii **Is capital punishment the best punishment for murderers and terrorists?**
Discuss the arguments for and against capital punishment.

13 **Discussion sections in research reports**

The term *discussion* has a variety of meanings in English. In academic writing, however, it usually refers to two types of activity:

a) considering both sides of an issue or question,
b) considering the results of research and the implications of these.

Discussion sections in research reports are the most complex in terms of their elements.

The short extract below comes from the **discussion section** of a dissertation in the field of Linguistics. With a partner, work out what the writer is trying to do in each sentence.

a) The other interesting finding was that the scientific corpus* analysed in this study contained a much lower density of modal verbs than the large general English corpora* studied by Evans (2001) and analysed by Morley (1998).

b) This is undoubtedly because the range of modal meanings appropriately conveyed in science writing, and possibly in some other types of academic writing, is in some ways more restricted than in many other written varieties.

c) Nevertheless, the high frequencies of the modal verbs may and can in the scientific corpora compared with the two general English corpora are interesting exceptions.

d) There are probably certain uses of may and can that are characteristic of scientific and possibly other academic texts, while some of the meanings of will, would, could and should are less appropriate in scientific writing than in some other kinds of written English.

* corpus/plural corpora = collection(s) of texts

14 **Matching exercise**
Match the words on the left with suitable words on the right to form grammatically correct phrases/sentences which might be used in discussion sections.

a These findings of the current study are consistent	**i** been reported in the literature.
b It is therefore likely	**ii** with those of Smith and Jones (2001) who found ...
c From the above	**iii** it can be concluded that ...
d A strong relationship between X and Y has	**iv** that such connections exist between ...

15 **Matching exercise**

Match the words on the left with suitable words on the right to form grammatically correct phrases/sentences which might be used in discussion sections.

a	In contrast to earlier findings, however,	**i**	topic are therefore recommended.
b	The reason for this is not	**ii**	significant difference between ...
c	Further studies on the current	**iii**	no evidence of X was detected.
d	Contrary to expectations, this study did not find a	**iv**	clear but it may have something to do with ...

16 **Matching exercise**

Now match the completed phrases in both Exercises 14 and 15 with these functional headings.

a	Giving background information	**e**	Giving an explanation
b	Reference to previous research (support)	**f**	Suggesting a hypothesis
c	Reference to previous research (contradict)	**g**	Drawing a conclusion
d	Stating an unexpected outcome	**h**	Suggestions for future work

Figure 9.1. Plato and Aristotle from Raphael's painting The School of Athens. In 387 BC, Plato founded the Academy in Athens, the institution often described as the first European university. It provided a comprehensive curriculum, including such subjects as astronomy, biology, mathematics, political theory and philosophy.

17 Useful phrases for discussion sections of research reports

Background information
A strong relationship between X and Y has been reported in the literature.
In reviewing the literature, no data was found on the association between X and Y.
This study set out with the aim of assessing the importance of X in ...
The third question in this research was ...

Statements of result (usually with reference to results section)
The results of this study show/indicate that ...
This experiment did not detect any evidence for ...
The results of this study did not show that ...
Several regions of X exhibited ...

Unexpected outcome
Surprisingly, X was found to ...
One unanticipated finding was that ...
It is somewhat surprising that no X was noted in this condition ...
Contrary to expectations, this study did not find a significant difference between ...

Reference to previous research (support)
These findings of the current study are consistent with those of ...
This finding supports previous research into this area which ...
These findings further support the idea of ...
These results are consistent with other studies and suggest that ...

Explanations
A possible explanation for this might be that ...
It is difficult to explain this result, but it might be related to ...
The reason for this is not clear but it may have something to do with ...
This inconsistency may be due to / could be attributed to ...

Suggesting hypotheses
This suggests that ...
It is possible/likely/probable, therefore, that ...
Hence, it could conceivably be hypothesised that ...
These findings suggest that ...

Conclusions
From the above it can be concluded that ...
In general, therefore, it seems that ...
It is possible, therefore, that ...
It can, therefore, be assumed that the ...

Suggestions for further research
Further research should be done to investigate the ...
Research questions that could be asked include ...
Further studies on the current topic are therefore recommended.
A further study with more focus on X is therefore suggested.

1 Pre-reading

- Draw a rice plant and label its parts. What do you know about the rice growing process? Share your ideas/drawings with your partner or class.
- Order these words so that they correspond to the stages in the rice growing process.

raking   harrowing   threshing   ripening   winnowing   ploughing   planting   harvesting

2 Reading

Read the text. Underline the verb forms and adverbs that are used. What type are they?

(1) Traditional methods of preparing land for wet rice vary with local custom, the nature of the soil and the water supply. In many places, the land is first flooded and then thoroughly cultivated with oxen or buffaloes, using implements which vary in number and kind with locality. The first operation is usually ploughing, and this may be repeated several times and accompanied by

5   raking in order to incorporate crop residues and to bury or remove weeds. Various kinds of harrows are then used, together with the trampling of animals, to puddle the flooded soil and bring it to the consistency of creamy mud in order to make the land suitable for the reception of seed or seedlings and to reduce the loss of drainage water. Finally, the water depth may be reduced to 2 cm or 3 cm and the land surface made smooth with a plank of wood pulled by an

10 ox or buffalo.

(2) In some places, for example in Sri Lanka and parts of India, it is customary to sow seed in the field, either into dry soil, or onto soft mud under a thin skin of water. In most places, however, rice seedlings, which have been raised in nurseries for 5 or 6 weeks, are transplanted into puddled fields. The seedlings are easily placed into holes made with a stick or by hand.

15 **(3)** After planting, weeds are usually controlled by pulling them out by hand, but in some places harrows are used. The land normally remains flooded until after the rice has flowered, when the water is gradually drained off to facilitate the ripening and harvesting of the crop. Harvesting is almost universally done by hand and in some places each ear is cut off separately by hand, partly because of the uneven ripening of many of the older indigenous varieties and partly on

20 account of superstitions. In other areas, however, sickles have customarily been employed and their use is becoming much more widespread with the introduction of more evenly ripening varieties. Threshing may be done by hand using a method of beating the crop against a ladder or screen or the grain may be trodden out by animals. Winnowing is usually done by the age-old method of throwing the threshed material into the air and allowing the wind to separate the chaff

25 from the grain.

3 Information extraction and summary

Reorder the following prompts, then write out a short summary of the traditional rice growing process below. The first sentence has been written out for you.

a		harvested crop ... threshed ... winnowed
b		the seedlings ... transplanted
c		weeds ... controlled
d		most places ... rice ... harvested by hand
e		the land ... flooded ... cultivated
f		water ... drained off

i)   *The land is first flooded then thoroughly cultivated using oxen or buffaloes.*

ii)   ....

iii)   ....

iv)   ....

v)   ....

vi)   ....

Figure 10.1. Transplanting rice seedlings in Bali.

4 Language for describing processes

Sequence adverbs

The land is first flooded and then thoroughly cultivated ...

First Next Finally	the fields are flooded. the water depth may be reduced.

Sequence adjectives + nouns

The	first next final	operation is usually ploughing. stage of the process is winnowing.

Sequence prepositions

After Before	planting, weeds are usually ... transplanting, the seedlings are grown in nurseries. this stage, ... that, ...

Clauses with 'when', 'after', 'before', and 'until'

The land normally remains flooded until after the rice has flowered, when the water is gradually drained off ...
Before the seedlings are planted, the soil is brought to the consistency of creamy mud.

Passive verb constructions[1] + with/..using ...

The land is first flooded and then thoroughly cultivated[2] with oxen ... using implements which ...

Passive verb constructions + by doing ...

After planting, weeds are usually controlled by pulling them out by hand ...

Infinitive of purpose

... and this may be repeated several times ... in order to incorporate crop residues ...
Various kinds of rollers are then used ... to puddle the flooded soil ... in order to render the land suitable for ...

1   *Tend to be used when the agent (doer) of an action is obvious from context and where the focus is on the verb (action) and its object.*
2   *Notice how two main verbs may share the same auxiliary ("is")*

5 Gap-fill exercise

The text below describes another rice growing process. This time you have to write the correct form of the verb in brackets, using either the passive form or the active form.

An example of extreme energy consumption for food production is processed cereal foods made from rice grown in California. The rice paddies **1) (first prepare)** .... using heavy tractors and grading equipment. Maximum efficiency is realised if the field is absolutely flat. Therefore, the most mechanised farms **2) (use)** .... a laser-computer levelling system. A rotating laser transmitter **3) (first establish)** .... in the centre of the field. This device beams an electronic reference elevation. A tractor **4) (then drag)** .... a levelling plough with a laser receiver mounted above it. A small computer on the tractor **5) (determine)** .... whether the elevation of the field at any point is above or below the required reference level. The computer **6) (then operate)** .... a motor which raises or lowers the levelling blades behind the tractor. Fertilizer **7) (apply)** .... heavily. Water, piped in from hundreds of kilometres away, is used to flood the fields. Rice seeds, previously treated with chemicals to control seedling diseases, **8) (spread)** .... by aeroplane. Further aerial spraying of pesticides and herbicides protects the crop, which **9) (finally harvest)** .... by large combines.

Growing and harvesting is only a first step. The rice **10) (then clean)** ...., **11) (mill)** .... to remove the nutritious outer hull, **12) (refortify)** .... with vitamins to replace some of the removed nutrients, and then puffed, blown, cooked, packaged and transported to produce cold cereal products or snack foods available on a supermarket shelf. The efficiency of the entire process **13) (depend)** .... on how you look at it. In terms of total yield (kilogram of grain per hectare of land), U.S. rice culture is nearly twice as efficient as the world average. However, in terms of energy input to energy output, the system is terribly inefficient. In the entire process, approximately five calories of fossil fuel energy **14) (need)** .... to produce one calorie of food energy.

6 Discussion

What do you think are the wider implications of the extensive agricultural methods described in the passage above?

Figure 10.2. Harvesting wheat in Nebraska, USA.
An example of an energy intensive agriculture system.

7 Writing task

Use the information in the following flow diagram to write a simple description of the process involved in the production and supply of petrol.

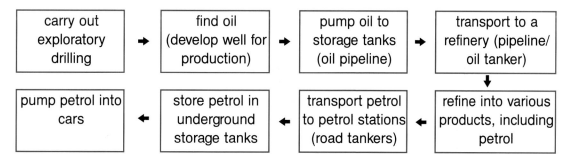

8 Use of the passive voice
Study the following transformations. Why would a writer make such transformations?

a	The researcher divided the rats into four groups. The rats were divided into four groups.
b	Aerosol sprays have damaged the ozone layer. The ozone layer has been damaged by aerosol sprays.
c	Students should submit their assignments before the 12th December. Assignments should be submitted before the 12th December.
d	The doctor will have to give him a course of antibiotics. He will have to be given a course of antibiotics.
e	The government is considering new measures to combat crime. New measures to combat crime are being considered.
f	The student should have checked the apparatus before conducting the experiment. The apparatus should have been checked before the experiment was conducted.

9 Transformation exercise
Transform the following sentences from active to passive leaving out the agent where it is unnecessary.

a The Department will reorganise the degree programmes to fit the new modular courses.

....

b Engineers can machine most metals into precise dimensions.

....

c They are going to hold this year's Biennial Conference at Nottingham University.

....

d The research assistant should have checked the research data more thoroughly.

....

e Demographers then use the information to predict population change over time.

....

f Scientists classify impurities in water as suspended, colloidal or dissolved.

....

10 Writing Task
Write a short text describing a process that you are familiar with, e.g. treating a patient, developing a drug, carrying out a survey and analysing the data, developing a computer programme, preparing a chemical agent, analysing a text, developing a course, passing a law, marketing a product. You will need to use both active and passive forms.

11 **Describing research methods: matching exercises**

In the Methods section of a dissertation or research report, writers give an account of how they carried out their research. Unlike in the previous texts, a specific process that took place at a particular time is described and so the simple past tense is usually used. The Methods section should be clear and detailed enough for another experienced person to repeat the research and reproduce the results.

(i) **Can you match the headings in the box with the sets of phrases below? The phrases have been taken from student dissertations at the University of Manchester.**

Common moves/functions in methods sections:
1 Describing some of the main methods used in the discipline
2 Giving reasons why a particular method was adopted
3 Indicating sample size and characteristics
4 Indicating sequence

a		All of the participants were aged between 18 and 19 at the beginning of the study ... Two groups of subjects were interviewed, namely X and Y. A random sample of patients with X was recruited from ...
b		*Prior to* commencing the study, ethical clearance was sought from ... *After collection*, the samples were shipped back to X in sealed containers. *Following this*, the samples were recovered and stored overnight at ...
c		The semi-structured approach was chosen because ... Smith *et al.* (1994) identify several advantages of the case study, ... It was decided that the best method to adopt for this investigation was to ...
d		To date various methods have been developed and introduced to measure X. In most recent studies, X is measured in four different ways. Radiographic techniques are the main non-invasive method used to determine X.

(ii)   Now match the headings in this box with the sets of phrases below.

Common moves/functions in methods sections
5   Indicating purpose
6   Indicating manner
7   Indicating tools or instruments used
8   Indicating problems or limitations

e		15 subjects were recruited using email advertisements requesting healthy students ... Statistical significance was analysed using analysis of variance and t-tests as appropriate. The data was recorded on a digital audio recorder and transcribed using a ...
f		To control for bias, measurements were carried out by another person. In order to identify the T10 and T11 spinous processes, the subjects were asked to ... In an attempt to make each interviewee feel as comfortable as possible, the interviewer ...
g		In this investigation there are several sources for error. The main error is ... Another major source of uncertainty is in the method used to calculate X. It was not possible to further investigate the significant relationships of X and Y because ...
h		The resulting solution was gently mixed at room temperature for ten minutes and ... A sample of the concentrate was then carefully injected into ... The tubes were accurately reweighed to six decimal places using ...

12 Procedural verbs

In describing research procedures certain verbs are frequently used. The list of verbs in the box below (left) has some of the more common procedural verbs used in science and social science subjects. Which of the nouns on the right collocate with them?

Verbs	Nouns
carried out	results
conducted	survey
noted	apparatus
set up	responses
observed	subjects
tabulated	instruments
interviewed	data
selected	experiment
obtained	interviews
recorded	research

Can you think of any more procedural verbs/nouns?

13 **Gap-fill exercise**
Use the words and phrases below to complete the gaps in the sentences that follow. These sentences have also been taken from student dissertations. More than one answer may be possible.

for the purpose of	*in order to*	*sources of error*	*carefully*
in an attempt	*prior to*	*once*	
then	*several advantages*	*were carried out*	

1 .... to make each interviewee feel as comfortable as possible, the interviewer began with ...
2 Independent tests .... on the x and y scores for the four years from ...
3 .... commencing the study, ethical clearance was sought from ...
4 .... height measurement, subjects were asked to stand ...
5 In this investigation there are several .... The main error is ...
6 Smith *et al.* (1994) identify .... of the case study, ...
7 .... identify the T10 and T11 spinous processes, the subjects were asked to ...
8 .... the exposures were completed, the X was removed from the Y and placed in ...
9 A sample of the concentrate was then .... injected into ...
10 The results were corrected for the background readings and .... averaged before being converted to ...

14 **Writing Task**
Proposed Research: If you are going to carry out a research project you should have an idea of the procedure you hope to follow.

Write a short account of this procedure. As the procedure has not been carried out yet, you should write it in the future tense (will + verb/will be + verb + ed).

1 **Introductory task**

One important characteristic of academic writing is that all the sources of information that the writer has used need to be indicated, not just as a bibliography or list of references, but also in or alongside the text.

In each of the extracts below, which have been taken from a range of academic disciplines, reference is made to an original source or sources. Study the extracts and complete the following tasks.

i)   Note how and where reference is made to the original source.
ii)   Identify the reporting verbs where they are used.
iii)   Note the tenses used in reporting. Can you identify any patterns in the use of tenses?

a In the 1950s Gunnar Myrdal pointed to some of the ways in which the prevailing assumptions of economic theory precluded an adequate understanding of underdevelopment ... (Myrdal, 1957).

b A relationship exists between an individual's working memory and their ability to suppress intrusive thoughts or behaviours (Rosen and Eagle, 1998).

c This experiment, by Kaye and Pearce (1984) (see also Pearce, Kaye, and Mall, 1982), included a group of rats which were given a series of presentations of a light, a stimulus that initially evoked a behavioural response.

d While some limited research with ground squirrels has indicated that animals who give alarm calls are most likely to be taken (Halliday, 1979; Smith and Frawley, 1983), this study does not support such results.

e In yet another major study, Mincer (1974) found that just over half of the inequality in earnings can be explained in terms of inequality in the educational attainment.

f Eysenck (1975) shows through extended case studies how experts deal with the complex problems which arise in the course of therapy.

g MIF has also been shown to reverse the anti-inflammatory effects of glucocorticoids in murine-induced arthritis (11).

Figure 11.1. Karl Marx in 1872.

h In the final part of the *Theses*, Marx writes: 'Philosophers have hitherto only interpreted the world in various ways; the point is to change it.' [23]

2 Reference systems used in academic writing

i) The system used in examples a) to f) above is now the most common and is known as the Harvard author/date system. Full bibliographical details of each source are listed in a bibliography or list of references at the end of the text.

ii) In example g), the system used is that a number is given in brackets (11) for each source, and full bibliographical references are then listed in number order at the end of the text.

iii) In example h), the superscript number [23] is a footnote number and a full bibliographical reference is given at the foot of the page. A bibliography is also given at the end of the text.

N.B. (i) Although different academic disciplines each have their preferred referencing system, most use one of the above systems.

(ii) Throughout this unit almost all the examples and exercises use the Harvard in-text referencing system.

(iii) See the bibliography on p. 109 of this book for a sample bibliography.

3 Reporting patterns (1)

When you refer to the work of other authors, you may choose to focus either on the *information* provided by that author, or on the author *him/herself*.

Which of the following examples are a) information prominent or b) author prominent?

1 For viscoelastic fluids, the behaviour of the time-dependent stresses in the transient shear flows is also very important (Boger et al., 1974).

2 Close (1983) developed a simplified theory using an analogy between heat and mass transfer and the equivalent heat transfer case.

3 Several authors have suggested that automated testing should be more readily accepted (Balcer, 1989; Stahl, 1989; Carver and Tai, 1991).

4 Lockhart (1999) argues that German society, like others, is not composed of a single national character or culture.

5 A number of investigators have demonstrated that cultural orientations help to explain prominent instances of political change such as revolutions (Taylor, 1989; Goldstone, 1991; Foran, 1997).

Now re-read the examples given in *1. Introductory task* and identify the reporting pattern used in each case. Is it author or information prominent?

4 Reporting verbs: matching exercise
Below are some of the more common verbs used to report what other people have written or said. Match the verbs on the left with the meanings on the right.

argue	**a** to draw someone's attention to a fact or a mistake
mention	**b** to refer briefly to something or somebody, in spoken or written text
conclude	**c** to say that something is true or correct and give reasons for this
point out	**d** to offer a plausible explanation for something
suggest	**e** to decide that something is true using the facts you have as a basis

Now match the next group of verbs to their meanings.

claim	**a** to hold certain views or opinions strongly even if other people disagree
show	**b** to say that something is true or correct while firm evidence for this may be lacking
maintain	**c** to discover or notice the existence of something
state	**d** to give information about something which is clear and convincing to other people
identify	**e** to write or say something in a formal and certain way

Most of the verbs studied above are usually followed by that + subject + verb. However, two of the verbs tend to be followed by a noun or noun phrase (N/NP). Which are they?

5 **Use of reporting verbs**

Reporting verbs are used to introduce paraphrases and summaries of other people's ideas in writing.

i) **Put the list of reporting verbs below into two groups: one for describing an idea, the second for giving an opinion about someone's idea.**

suggest   argue   claim   identify   list   maintain   mention   point out   conclude

ii) **Can you think of any other reporting verbs to add to each group?**

iii) **Three of the words above are given with each of the quotations below. Choose one of the three to paraphrase or report the quotation. Where more than one choice is possible, decide on the best.**

Example

'Studying in an English speaking country seems to be one of the best methods of improving your English language' (Farrelly, 1989: 43).

i. **lists**   ii. **suggests**   iii. **identifies**

Answer

Farrelly (1989: 43) suggests that studying in an English speaking country seems to be one of the best methods of improving your English language.

a 'There are three reasons why the English language has become so dominant. These are: ...' (Maynard, 1993: 137).

i. mentions   **ii.** lists   **iii.** claims

b 'Despite some recent evidence to the contrary, I still believe that many heart attacks could be avoided with very limited changes in exercises and eating habits' (Mawali, 1999: 32).

i. maintains   **ii.** argues   **iii.** concludes

c 'Poor food, bad housing, inadequate hygiene and large families are the major causes of infant mortality' (Popper and Friedman, 1991: 77).

i. mention   **ii.** point out   **iii.** identify

d 'It is worth noting that gardening has always been an effective therapy for those with depressive tendencies' (Armani, 1983: 72).

      i. maintains   **ii.** concludes   **iii.** points out

e 'When the mother tongue is banned from the classroom, the teaching tends to lead to the alienation of the students. This is because … ' (Sargnagel, 1993: 20).

      i. suggests   **ii.** argues   **iii.** identifies

f 'Curative medicine has ensured great health improvements in developed countries. Nevertheless, preventative medicine is far more cost effective, and therefore better adapted to the developing world' (Carrow *et al.,* 1990: 32).

      i. list   **ii.** maintain   **iii.** conclude

g 'As a comparison, let me briefly refer to the great Persian poet, Rumi. In the Ma'navi, … ' (Carter, 1981: 99).

      i. mentions   **ii.** identifies   **iii.** argues

h 'By analysing the colour of the eye, a range of illnesses can be diagnosed and treated' (Bastien, 1998: 67).

      i. suggests   **ii.** lists   **iii.** claims

6 **Reporting research activity**

i) **Think of three ways in which the verbs below differ from the reporting verbs that we have just studied. Consider tense, sentence structure, meaning and collocation.**

investigate   find   examine   review   report   study   test   analyse   survey

ii) **Can you think of any other verbs that could be added?**

iii) **Complete the following sentences with the above verbs. In some cases more than one can be used. Use the past simple tense.**

a Tilak (1968) .... that as levels of literacy and education of the population in an economy rise, population below the poverty line decreases.

b Harbison (1977) .... the differential impact of formal and non-formal types of education on income distribution.

c Agarwal (1990) .... the data from 72 countries and concluded that there was a strong correlation between HDI and economic development.

d Thirty years later, Van den Bossche (1974) .... three cases of Candida Albicans which were resistant to treatment.

e Jencks (1989) .... the literature from the period and found little evidence for this claim.

f Shaw (1999) .... 250 undergraduate students using semi-structured questionnaires.

g Kibbler *et al.* (1979) .... the effects of Cytochrome P450 on unprotected nerve cells.

7 **Reporting patterns**
Statements reporting research tend to fall into one of three major patterns.

a)   Match each example with its tense and pattern.

Example	Tense	Pattern
I. Lightbown and Spada (1993) studied the differences between adult and child second language learners.	**a** Present	**i.** Focus on area of research – researchers mentioned
II. The differences between adult and child second language learners have been widely studied (Brown, 1973; Krashen, 1988; Lightbown and Spada (1993).	**b** Past	**ii.** Focus on what is known – no reference to research activity
III. The differences between adult and child second language learners are very significant (Brown, 1973; Krashen, 1988; Lightbown and Spada, 1993).	**c** Present Perfect	**iii.** Single study – researchers are subject – research activity mentioned in verb

b)   Match each example with its area and pattern.

Example	Area	Pattern
I. The differences between adult and child second language learners were studied by Lightbown and Spada (1993).	**a** Reference to areas of enquiry	**i.** The focus is on what is known
II. There have been several studies of the differences between adult and child second language learners (Brown, 1973; Krashen, 1988; Lightbown and Spada (1993).	**b** Reference to state of current knowledge	**ii.** Attention is given to what previous researchers did
III. There are very significant differences between adult and child second language learners (Brown, 1973; Krashen, 1988; Lightbown and Spada (1993).	**c** Reference to a single study	**iii.** Attention is given to what has been done

Thus the three most common reporting patterns are:

I. a. Lightbown and Spada (1993) *studied* the differences between adult and child second language learners.
   b. The differences between adult and child second language learners *were studied* by Lightbown and Spada (1993).

- Simple past tense
- Researcher is subject (or agent if the verb is passive)
- Research activity mentioned in verb
- Reference to single studies
- Attention to what a previous researcher did

II. a. The differences between adult and child second language learners *have been* widely *studied* (Brown, 1973; Krashen, 1988; Lightbown and Spada, 1993).
   b. There *have been* several studies of the differences between adult and child second language learners (Brown, 1973; Krashen, 1988; Lightbown and Spada, 1993).

- Present perfect tense
- Focus on area of research/enquiry
- Researchers mentioned in brackets
- Attention to what has been done

III. a. The differences between adult and child second language learners are very significant (Brown, 1973; Krashen, 1988; Lightbown and Spada, 1993).
   b. There are very significant differences between adult and child second language learners (Brown, 1973; Krashen, 1988; Lightbown and Spada, 1993).

- Present tense
- Focus on what is known
- No reference to research activity
- Reference to state of current knowledge

Notes

1. The use of the present perfect tense and the present tense to report research shows that the writer considers the research to be still relevant or current.
2. Where a writer wishes to refer to what an individual *wrote, thought, stated, concluded, claimed, argued, suggested,* etc., especially where a text of current interest or current relevance is being discussed, the present tense is frequently used. This occurs quite regularly in social science and humanities texts especially where quotations are given, even if the authors are clearly no longer alive. It is also frequently used with very well-known historical sources.

Smith's (1988) cross-country analysis concludes that literacy is positively correlated with economic development.

In the final part of the *Theses*, Marx writes: 'Philosophers have hitherto only interpreted the world in various ways; the point is to change it'.[23]

Plato begins the *Republic* with a Socratic conversation about the nature of justice, and then discusses the virtues of justice, wisdom, courage and moderation.

8 Writing Task

The following text uses only one referring pattern: author prominent and past simple tense. Rewrite the passage using a wider range of patterns. Also indicate that the work of Micheli and Elegem is still of current relevance.

Scheuermann's kyphosis is a condition in which the normal roundback in the upper spine (called a kyphosis) is increased. This condition occurs when the vertebrae become wedge-shaped, with the narrow part of the wedge in front. It has been found to be more common in athletes than non-athletes. Using X rays, Sward *et al.* (1992) demonstrated a high incidence of spinal abnormalities associated with Scheuermann's kyphosis in competitive athletes aged between 14 and 25. Endler *et al.* (1980) studied the thoracic curvature of 85 rowers and found symptoms of this kind of deformity in 68% of them. These researchers claimed that adolescent rowers experience this condition from constant stress on the lower sections of the spine. Tutsch *et al.* (1984) found a high incidence of thoracic deformity in competitive gymnasts (25%). Micheli (1985) suggested that this condition in gymnasts may be associated with repetitive flexion. Elegem (1983) reported that time pedalling in a bent position is associated with this condition in competitive cyclists. Stinton (1996) detected this condition in weightlifters and argued that the condition can result from excessive loading. Agarwal (1979) reported that in a study of 25 weightlifters, 44% exhibited angle deformity to the lower edges of the vertebrae.

9 Review of reporting tenses: gap-fill exercise

Complete these sentences using a verb form which you feel is the most acceptable. In some cases more than one form is possible.

a Recent investigations .... **(indicate)** that there may be a relationship between the new drug and liver cancer (Smith, 1992; Jones, 1995).

b Smith (1998) .... **(find)** that a diet of GM tomatoes resulted in high level of aggression in mice.

c Current research shows that GM varieties of maize .... **(be)** able to cross-pollinate with non-GM varieties (Smith, 2004; Jones, 2005).

d Jones (2005) .... **(argue)** that the environmental dangers of GM crops have not been thoroughly considered.

e The relationship between a diet high in fats and poor health .... widely **(investigate)** (Smith, 1985; Jones, 1987; Johnson, 1992).

f There .... **(be)** an unambiguous relationship between spending on education and economic development (Blunkett, 2005).

g O'Brien (1978) .... **(study)** the relationship between literacy levels and economic development.

h It .... **(demonstrate)** that a high intake of GM starch, over a long period of time, results in damage to vital organs in rats (Smith, 1987; Jones, 1992; Johnson, 1998).

i In *The Turning Point*, Fritjof Capra .... **(highlight)** the recent changes in attitudes in biology, physics, medicine and economics which he attributes to 'a developing new consciousness ...' [93]

10 Extended tasks

1) Select a piece of your own writing, such as a current assignment or study project, and check your use of reporting verbs and referencing conventions.

2) Find three academic papers from three different journals related to your discipline, e.g. journals available in your library or on the Internet. Write a short report which describes the referencing systems used in each journal. Make sure you list the three journals in a *List of References*.

11 **Consolidation: matching exercise**

Match the following headings with the phrases in the boxes below. The phrases were all found in native speaker dissertations.

- Reference to what other writers do in their text: author as subject
- General descriptions of the relevant literature
- Reference to current state of knowledge
- Reference to single investigations in the past: investigation prominent
- General reference to previous studies/research
- Reference to single investigations in the past: research topic as subject
- Reference to single investigations in the past: researcher as sentence subject

---

A A number of controlled studies *have suggested* that ... (Smith, 1996; Jones 1999; Johnson, 2001).

Recently, in vitro studies *have shown* that T.thermophylus EFTu can ... (Patel *et al.*, 1997; ...).

Several attempts *have been made* to ... (Smith, 1996; Jones 1999; Johnson, 2001).

Several studies *have revealed* that it is not just X that acts on ... (Smith, 1996; Jones ...).

B Smith and West *performed* a similar series of experiments in the 1960s to show that ...

Smith and Shaw (1993) *carried out* a number of investigations into the ...

Zhao (1995) *conducted* a series of trials in which he mixed X with different quantities of ...

Yavary *et al.*[8] *measured* both components of the ...

C Preliminary work on X was *undertaken* by Karim (1992).

Analysis of the genes involved in X was *first carried* out by Smith *et al.* (1983).

A recent study by Smith and Jones (2001) *involved* ...

A longitudinal study of X by Smith (2002) *reported* that ...

D Smith (2003) *identifies* poor food, bad housing and large families as the major causes of ...

Rao (2003) *lists* three reasons why the English language has become so dominant.

Smith (2003) *traces* the development of Japanese history and philosophy during the 19th century.

Jones (2003) *provides* in-depth analysis of the work of Aristotle showing its relevance to ...

E A considerable amount of literature *has been published* on X. These studies ...

The first serious discussions and analyses of X *emerged* during the 1970s with ...

The generalisability of much published research on this issue *is* problematic.

What we know about X *is largely based* upon empirical studies that investigate how ...

F Classic conditioning *was first demonstrated* experimentally by Pavlov (Smith, 2002).

The electronic spectroscopy of X *was first studied* by Smith and Douglas in 1970.

The acid-catalyzed condensation reaction between X and Y *was first reported* by Baeyer in 1872.

X *was originally isolated* from Y in a soil sample from ... (Wang *et al.*, 1952).

G MIF *reverses* the effects of X (Patel, 2005).

A relationship *exists* between X and Y ... (Jones *et al.*,1998).

GM varieties of maize *are able* to cross-pollinate with ... (Smith, 1998; Jones, 1999).

There *is* an unambiguous relationship A and B ... (Rao, 1998).

1 **Pre-reading**

a) What do you know about the differences between male and female speech? Do males ask more questions than females? Why?/Why not?

b) Discuss the meanings of the following words with your partner:

coerce   persuasive   tag questions   status-marked settings   accusatory

2 **Reading**

Read the text below to find out what recent research has to say on the question in a).

The Use of Questions

(1) Many studies of male and female speech have found women using more questions than men especially when the addressee is a man. For instance, women were found to ask more questions than men when buying tickets at Central Station in Amsterdam, especially when the ticket seller was male (Brouwer *et al.*, 1979). And in a detailed study of three separate
5   heterosexual couples based on fifty-two hours of tape-recorded conversation in their homes, Fishman (1983) found that the women asked a staggering two and a half times more questions than the men did. Fishman sees this as a practical measure of the work these women were doing to keep conversations going. Women made sixty-two percent of all attempts to introduce topics but only thirty-eight per cent of these attempts achieved joint development. Conversely,
10 nearly all the topics initiated by men (usually in the form of a statement) were taken up in the conversation. Thus, on the one hand, women responded more positively to topics raised by men; and on the other hand, they had to work harder to establish topics themselves, which required them to use more questions.

(2) This kind of finding seems fairly clear cut and can be used to support claims that women
15 are more attentive in their talk to the needs and rights of others. However, Fishman makes no attempt to differentiate between various different types of question: her conclusions would have been more persuasive if she had discussed in more detail whether different types of question might not have been at work in her data and what criteria might be used to identify them. For questions are not all of the same kind, nor do they all perform the same function in
20 conversation: not all of them necessarily work to support and sustain topical development. A questioner, for instance, may claim, confirm, or even challenge a power relation by their use. Tag questions, for example, may be either facilitative and oriented towards the addressee, i.e. their function is to help the conversation along by offering a speaking turn to another participant, for example:

> *'That was a good film, wasn't it?'*

25 or checking and therefore speaker-oriented (i.e. making sure about something), for example:

> *'You came to Glasgow last year, didn't you?'*

Their meaning can also differ according to context. For example, in asymmetrical status-marked settings, such as the classroom or, for example, the courtroom, tags similar in formal construction to those of the facilitative type seem to take on a different force. They quite
30 typically operate to coerce agreement from the addressee in some negative assessment of their behaviour. Consider, for instance:

> *'This homework isn't very good, is it?'* [teacher to pupil]
> *'You're not making much of an effort to pay off these arrears, are you?'*
> [magistrate to defendant]

35 Thus, the same construction as that adopted for facilitative tags can well become coercive, even accusatory, in particular circumstances.

3 Intensive reading
According to the text are the following statements True (T) or False (F)?

a A study carried out in Amsterdam in 1979 showed that rail ticket sellers asked more questions when the passengers were female.	**T/F**
b Another study showed that at home women asked two and half times more questions than men.	**T/F**
c It seems that women make a greater effort to keep conversations going.	**T/F**
d One of the functions of tag questions is to help conversations along.	**T/F**
e Speakers sometimes use tag questions to accuse the listener.	**T/F**

4 Critical reading: some questions to ask
Here are some useful questions to ask when evaluating a research report.

i) What is the key evidence used to support the argument?
ii) Has all the necessary evidence been given or are there some gaps in the information provided? Is the evidence relevant and sufficient to support the conclusion?
iii) Does the evidence come from a reputable, up-to-date source?
iv) Is the evidence interpreted correctly?
v) Does the conclusion follow logically from the evidence or would another conclusion be possible?
vi) Is the conclusion too general and not fully supported by the evidence?
vii) Are any statistics or data misleading?
viii) Does the writer show any bias or have any hidden assumptions? For example, has the writer been sponsored by an organisation?

Re-read the first paragraph of the text and answer the above questions. Do you have any criticisms of the reported research in addition to those given in paragraph 2?

5 Language focus
The writer of the text on the previous page identifies a flaw or weakness with certain research findings.
a) How is this weakness introduced?
b) What grammatical structure does the writer use to comment on the weakness?

6 Unreal conditions
Consider the grammatical form of the statement below:

> Her conclusions would have been more persuasive if she had discussed the different types of questions.

a) Make statements with a similar meaning using these prompts:

It ... have ... better if ...
The findings would ... more convincing if ...
The results ... useful if ...

b) What is the difference between the two sentences below?

> Your study project would have been considerably improved if you had given more examples.
>
> Your study project would be considerably improved if you gave more examples.

c) Now make similar conditional statements about yourself and about this course using these prompts:

My IELTS/TOEFL test score would have been higher if ...
The meeting with my tutor would have gone better if ...
My last presentation would have been better if ...
This course book would be/have been better if ...

d) What is the difference between the three sentences below?

> You should have given more examples in your study project.
>
> You could have given more examples in your study project.
>
> You might have given more examples in your study project.

7 Use of *however*

> *However* is a powerful word which is often used to draw attention to a problem. This may be a knowledge gap in a field of enquiry, a flaw or weakness in some previous research, or a weakness with a plan or project or idea.

What can you say about the function of *however* in the extracts below?

> However, the previously mentioned methods suffer from some serious limitations.
>
> However, the paper would appear to be over-ambitious in its claims.
>
> So far, however, very little research has been carried out on the impact of these policies.
>
> However, the tax increase resulting from this proposal would be politically unacceptable.

8 **Introducing questions, problems and limitations (theory)**
Match the phrases on the left with those on the right to make longer phrases.

a One question that needs to be	**i** is that it does not explain why ...
b A serious weakness	**ii** asked, however, is whether ...
c The key problem with this	**iii** with this argument, however, is that ...
d However, one of the limitations with this explanation	**iv** explanation is that ...

9 **Introducing questions, problems and limitations (method/practice)**
Match the phrases on the left with those on the right to make longer phrases or sentences.

a Another problem with this	**i** suffer from some serious limitations.
b Difficulties arise, however, when	**ii** approach is that it fails to take X into account ...
c However, all the previously mentioned methods	**iii** an attempt is made to implement the policy.
d Perhaps the most serious	**iv** disadvantage of this method is that ...

10 **Language for being critical**

Introducing problems and limitations

However, Fishman makes no attempt to differentiate between various different types ...

However, the previously mentioned methods suffer from some serious | limitations. / weaknesses. / drawbacks.

Another problem with this approach is that it fails to take X into account.
One of the limitations with this explanation is that it does not explain why ...
Difficulties arise, however, when an attempt is made to implement the policy.
The strategy has not escaped criticism from governments, agencies and academics.
The main weakness of the study, and it is a major one, is the failure to address how ...

Introducing other people's criticisms

Many analysts now argue that the strategy of X has not been successful.
Non-government agencies are also very critical of the new policies.

The X theory has been | vigorously / strongly | challenged in recent years by a number of writers.

Smith's analysis has been criticised by a number of writers. Jones (1993) for example, points out that ...
Smith is probably the best known critic of the X theory. He argues that ...

11 Evaluative adjectives
Do the following adjectives have a positive, negative or neutral value when used in the following construction?

In their .... study, Evans and Leech ...

important	*innovative*	*exploratory*	*rigorous*	*ambitious*
limited	*small scale*	*flawed*	*impressive*	*useful*
modest	*original*	*interesting*	*simple*	*preliminary*

12 Writing Task
Write about 200 words describing some research work that you have recently reviewed. Note its strengths and its weaknesses.

13 Discussion
In small groups, see if you can agree on three or four evaluative comments or criticisms of this course.

Figure. 12.1. Socrates (470-399BC) is famous for his willingness to call everything into question. He is said to be the first clear exponent of critical philosophy.

14 **Concluding exercises**
Read the following text taken from a non-academic source and then do the exercises which follow.

The dieters destined for failure

(1) It's something that most dieters will have experienced – losing all those pounds only to put them all back on later.

(2) Now doctors have discovered why it is so hard to maintain weight loss. It's all because of our hormones.

5 **(3)** A study looked at the effects of the hormone leptin, which plays a key role in regulating our metabolism and tells our body when it has had too much food.

(4) The researchers found that when we lose weight, our levels of leptin also fall, making it harder to burn off the calories and sending our weight creeping back up.

(5) The findings could explain why 85 per cent of dieters fail to keep to their target weight –
10 and could also pave the way for new leptin-based dieting drugs.

(6) Dr Michael Rosenbaum, who led the research funded by First Great Pharmaceuticals in New York, said the key to maintaining weight loss is to keep our leptin levels high.

(7) 'Anyone who has ever tried to lose weight knows that you never lose as much as you should for what you are eating,' he said.

15 **(8)** 'And even if you reach a weight you are happy with, you are never able to sustain that level of thinness.

(9) 'Leptin fools your body into being happy with a lower weight. It won't help you lose weight but it should help you keep weight off once you have lost it.'

(10) Dr Rosenbaum's team looked at the effect of leptin on healthy volunteers.

20 **(11)** As the men and women lost weight, their leptin levels fell. But giving them leptin allowed them to keep to their new weight, the study, published in a US journal, found.

(12) Previous studies have shown that leptin acts as an appetite suppressant.

(13) Research last year showed that when we don't get enough sleep, our levels of leptin fall and we feel the urge to eat more.

25 **(14)** Leptin is one of many chemicals released during sleep and it is thought that losing just an hour or two of sleep a night might be enough to cause a significant dip in levels of the hormone.

(15) The findings suggested those who regularly have too little sleep, such as night-shift workers, are at very high risk of becoming obese.

1) **Using the questions given in Ex. 4.** *Critical reading* **to help you, evaluate the above research report and then write a short text criticising it.**
2) **Working with a partner or in a small group, list some of the principal features of academic writing style.**
3) **Re-read the text above and make a list of the ways in which it differs from a typical academic text.**

The Academic Writing Process

What steps should a student writer go through between first receiving an academic writing assignment and finally submitting it? The following table lists some basic steps which many experienced academic writers find both helpful and productive.

STEP	PURPOSE
1 Analyse the question	To determine what material and topics need to be covered and in what way.
2 Brainstorm	To think deeply about the topic and establish what is already known (and not known) about it.
3 Prepare an initial outline	To formulate a preliminary structure and to highlight gaps in knowledge.
4 Research and Note taking	To find, evaluate and select essential relevant information. To paraphrase and summarise, as necessary, and to record clearly direct quotations for possible use.
	N.B. Accurate note taking and the recording of all necessary referencing/bibliographical information are essential aids for avoiding plagiarism.
5 Prepare a final outline	To refine and develop the initial outline in the light of research and new information. To shape all ideas and notes into a coherent, balanced and logical structure.
6 Write the first draft	
7 Revise the first draft	To improve the content, organisation and coherence. To correct errors of language, spelling and punctuation.
8 Write the second draft and additional drafts if necessary	To incorporate revisions into the text. Only selected parts may need re-drafting.
9 Prepare the final text	To incorporate all revisions, in-text references and Bibliography entries. To follow correct format as instructed e.g. double-spacing.
10 Proofread carefully	To find and correct any remaining errors.

Punctuation

As the purpose of punctuation is to make written English easier to read and to make the meaning clear and unambiguous, good, accurate punctuation is important in academic writing. The following notes highlight points of particular relevance to academic writing.

Full stop .

- To indicate the end of a sentence
- To indicate an abbreviation such as etc., *et al.* (not always used)
- To indicate an omission in a quoted text ...

Comma ,

- To separate long co-ordinate clauses joined by words such as *and, but, or*
- To separate a subordinate clause (beginning with words such as *although, when, because*) from the main clause, particularly if the subordinate clause comes first in the sentence
- To indicate additional information in a sentence
- To indicate a non-defining relative clause, *which simply provides additional information*, in a sentence
- To separate items in a list such as *clauses, phrases, nouns, adjectives* and *adverbs*

Semi-colon ;

- To separate two sentences that are very closely connected in meaning (optional, in place of a full stop): *Some students prefer to write essays; others prefer to give presentations.*
- To clearly separate items in a grammatically complex list. *There are daily demonstrations and incidents; students demand the ousting of Habibie, who is seen as the defender of the Suharto legacy; workers protest at price rises which make one meal a day a luxury; and the unemployed desperately seek work for themselves in the formal economy.*

Colon :

- To introduce an explanation: *The reason the experiment failed was obvious: the equipment was faulty.*
- To introduce a list, particularly a grammatically complex list: *see above example under semi-colon*
- To introduce a direct quotation, particularly a long one: *Jones (2003) states that:*

Quotation marks ‘ ’ / “ ”

- To indicate a direct quotation
- To highlight words or phrases used in a special or unusual way: *Quotation marks are also called 'inverted commas'.*

  N.B. Single quotation marks now seem to be more commonly used than double.

  N.B. For quotations within quotations, use double quotation marks inside single (or single inside double).

Dash —

Generally avoid in formal academic writing. Replace by colon, semi-colon, or brackets, as appropriate.

The Use of the Article

The use of articles in English is a very complex area. However, there are a few simple rules which will help you in many situations and these are explained below:

Singular countable nouns

All singular countable nouns are always preceded by a small modifying word known in grammar as a determiner, and this is often an article (*a/an, the*). Countable words include: *system, model, method, approach, group, problem, effect, level, investigation, sector, study*

Note that even if these words are preceded by uncountable nouns or adjectives a determiner is still needed: *the greenhouse effect, the transport system, the control group*
        a high level, a systematic approach, a rigorous study

Plural countable nouns

If the writer is thinking about a specific group, then the definite article is normally used:
The books in this collection were published in the 19th or early 20th century.

Otherwise no article is used:
Learners tend to remember new facts when they are contextualised.

Uncountable nouns

Uncountable nouns are not normally accompanied by an article.

Science has been defined as a systematic approach to answering questions.

But if they are post-modified by *of ...*, or *which ...* the definite article is normally used:

The science of global warming is a complex and controversial area.
Chemistry is the science which addresses the composition and behaviour of matter.

Names

Names and titles are not normally preceded by the definite article (*the*)

Manchester University, Manchester

But this changes if the noun phrase contains a post-modifying structure (*of ...*)

The University of Manchester; The United States of America

or, if they contain words like *organisation, association* or *institute*

The World Health Organisation, The American Heart Association, The Royal Society, The SETI Institute

Apart from these simple rules, the other thing you need to do is to check how noun phrases are used in the texts that you read. Make a mental note of this as you read, or check back to the source text when you are writing.

Commonly Confused Words

Your spell checker will only indicate words that are misspelt and which it does not recognise. However, if a misspelling results in a word which has another meaning or use, the spell checker will not show this to you. Here is a list of words which are commonly confused:

affect/effect
Affect is a verb. *Effect* is a noun and is therefore always used after an article/determiner ('an' or 'the'/this). e.g. *The weather can **affect** our mood. The **effect** of the weather on our mood is well known.*

compliment/complement
Compliment (verb) means to praise someone. *Complement* (verb) means to complete something in a way that makes it very good. Both words can also be used as nouns. e.g. *They **complimented** him on his success. There is always a written exam to **complement** the practical test.*

comprise/consist
Both words mean 'to be made up of', but only *consist* is accompanied by of. e.g. *The book **comprises** ten units. The exam **consists** of four parts.*

discrete/discreet
Discrete is an adjective which means 'separate' or 'distinct'. *Discreet* is an adjective which means 'to keep silent or be tactful about something'. e.g. *The instructions were written down in **discrete** steps. He was very **discreet** throughout the inspection.*

formerly/formally
Formerly means 'earlier'. *Formally* means 'conventionally' or 'officially'. e.g. *They had all **formerly** been students in the engineering department. They were all dressed **formally** for the graduation ceremony.*

its/it's
its – without an apostrophe - is a possessive determiner similar to 'my' or 'your'. *It's* is a contracted form of 'it is' or 'it has'. e.g. *The experiment was interesting but **its** outcome was predictable. **It's** the first step towards assimilation.*

later/latter
Later is an adverb which means 'at an advanced point of time'. *Latter* is an adjective used to refer to items in a text. It means 'more recently mentioned'. e.g. *They planned to merge the two departments at a **later** point. A word can acquire a more restricted sense or be chiefly used in one specialist field, the word doctor being a classic example of the **latter**.*

practice/practise
In British English, practice is a noun and practise is a verb. American English allows both spellings for both forms. e.g. *The more **practice** students get, the better their results will become. The more they **practise** evaluating texts, the more they will be able to identify flaws in research findings.*

precede/proceed
Precede means 'to come before'. *Proceed* means 'to go forward' or 'to begin to carry out'. e.g. *Any place offers will be **preceded** by interviews with department heads. Students are generally allowed to **proceed** with their research following approval of proposals from the head of department.*

principle/principal
Principle is a noun which means 'a basic belief, theory or rule'. *Principal* is an adjective which means 'main' or 'most important'. e.g. *The **principles** of quantum theory are not easily grasped. The **principal** reason for changes in the system is financial.*

there/their
There is used to indicate the existence of something. *Their* is used to indicate possession, i.e. if something belongs to someone or something. e.g. ***There** is only one way to achieve results. It was **their** determination that saved the day.*

British/US spelling

The most common difference which is noticed in academic writing concerns verbs which end in -ise (Br) or -ize (US):

analyse (Br) v analyze (US).
industrialise (Br) v industrialize (US).

This difference also affects the nouns derived from the verbs:
organisation (Br) v organization (US).

Another noticeable difference relates to words ending in -re:
centre (Br) v center (US).
metre (Br) v meter (US).

Here are some other differences:

British	US
aeroplane	airplane
behaviour	behavior
catalogue	catalog
colour	color
defence	defense
encyclopaedia	encyclopedia
foetus	fetus
instalment	installment
plough	plow
programme	program
sceptical	skeptical
skilful	skillful
travelled	traveled

Both spellings tend to be acceptable in most universities; however, writers need to be consistent in their use of one or the other.

Notes on sentence structure

Simple sentences
In written English all sentences contain a Subject - Verb structure
An electron (**S**) *is* (**V**) *an elementary particle.*

Various elements may be placed before or after the Subject - Verb structure:
Between 1933 and 1945, restrictions (**S**) *were placed* (**V**) *on German academics.*

These simple sentences always end in a full stop. In academic writing, however, many sentences are more complicated than this simple pattern.

Complex sentences
Many sentences contain more than one Subject - Verb structure, but one of these parts will convey the main meaning and will make sense by itself:
Even if a student is able to obtain the necessary funding, <u>there are other costs of studying abroad</u>.

Compound sentences
Some sentences may have two Subject - Verb structures and each of these convey meaning that can make sense by itself (two main parts). The two parts may be joined by words like *and, but, so,* or by using a semi-colon.
*Supporters of the 'Great Divide' theory agree that something is lost as well as gained when people become literate; **but** they consider it is worth losing some benefits in order to obtain many others.*

Common problems relating to sentence structure

Problems occur when:

- dependent parts of sentences are written as complete sentences with a full stop.
  *Even if a student is able to obtain the necessary funding. X

- two independent parts are written as one sentence without a conjunction.
  *Supporters of the 'Great Divide' theory agree that something is lost as well as gained when people become literate, they consider it is worth losing some benefits in order to obtain many others. X

Altbach, P.G. (1987) *The Knowledge Context: Comparative perspectives on the distribution of knowledge*, New York: State University of New York Press.

Altbach, P.G. (1990) 'Impact and adjustment: foreign students in comparative perspective', *Higher Education,* 21, 305-323.

Altbach, P.G. (2001) 'Academic Freedom: International realities and challenges', *Higher Education*, 41, 205-219.

Baldwin, P.J., Dodd, M. and Wrate, R.M. (1997) 'Young doctors' health – II. Health and health behaviour', *Social Science and Medicine*, 45 (1) 41-44.

Baugh, A.C. and Cable, T. (2002) *A History of the English Language*, 5th edition, London: Routledge.

Butterfield, C.H. (2003) 'The Effectiveness of Non-Governmental Organisations in Rural Poverty Alleviation in Uganda', Unpublished MSc thesis (Institute for Development Policy and Management), University of Manchester.

Clarke, D. (ed.) (1977) *A History of Inventions*, London: Cavendish.

Crystal, D. (1997) *The Cambridge Encyclopedia of Language*, 2nd edition, Cambridge: Cambridge University Press.

Fowles, J. (1994) 'Surface literacy, rooted orality: A hidden factor in teacher education in South Sulawesi'. Unpublished M.Ed. dissertation, The University of Manchester.

Krashen, S. (1988) *Second Language Acquisition and Second Language Learning*, Hemel Hempstead: Prentice Hall.

Lightbrown, P. and Spada, N. (1993) *How Languages are Learnt*, Oxford: Oxford University Press.

Lock, G. (1996) *Functional English Grammar: an introduction for second language teachers*, Cambridge: Cambridge University Press.

MacRae, F. (2005) 'The dieters destined for failure' *Daily Mail*, 2 December.

Millward, C.M. (1996) *A Biography of the English Language*, 2nd edition, London; New York: Holt, Rinehart and Winston.

Montgomery, M. and Reid-Thomas, H. (1994) *Language and Social Life*, London: The British Council.

Nawab, I.I., Speers, P.C. and Hoye, P.F. (eds), (1995) *Saudi Aramco and its World: Arabia and the Middle East*, Dhahran: Saudi Arabian Oil Company (Saudi Aramco).

Nunan, D. (1988) *The Learner Centred Curriculum*, Cambridge: Cambridge University Press.

Office of National Statistics (2005) *Social Trends*. www.statistics.gov.uk (correct on 12/12/05). np.

Rejabi, R. (2002). 'An investigation into sagittal thoracic curvature in cyclists and non-cyclists', Unpublished PhD thesis (Musculoskeletal Research Group), University of Manchester.

Time Life Books (1988) *Galaxies*, New York.

Turk, J. and Turk, A. (1984) *Environmental Science*, 3rd edition, New York: CBS College Publishing.

Webster, C.C. and Wilson, P.N. (1980) *Tropical Agriculture*, London: Longman.

Sources According to Units

EX. 1 From: Altbach, P.G. (1987) *The Knowledge Context: Comparative Perspectives on the Distribution of Knowledge*, New York: State University of New York Press, p. 131.

EX. 3 i) From: Millward, C.M. (1996) *A Biography of the English Language*, 2nd edition, London; New York: Holt, Rinehart and Winston, p. 345.

EX. 3 ii) From: Millward, C.M. (1996) *A Biography of the English Language*, 2nd edition, London; New York: Holt, Rinehart and Winston, p. 372.

EX. 3 iii) From: Baugh, A.C. and Cable, T. (2002) *A History of the English Language*, 5th edition, London: Routledge, p. 308.

EX. 3 iv) From: Rejabi, R. (2002) 'An investigation into sagittal thoracic curvature in cyclists and non-cyclists', Unpublished PhD thesis (Musculoskeletal Research Group, University of Manchester), p. 72.

EX. 4 From: Nawab, I.I., Speers, P.C. and Hoye, P.F. (eds), (1995) *Saudi Aramco and its World: Arabia and the Middle East*, Dhahran: Saudi Arabian Oil Company (Saudi Aramco), p.114.

EX. 6 From: Baugh, A.C. and Cable, T. (2002) *A History of the English Language*, 5th edition, London: Routledge, pp. 308-309.

Unit 2

EX. 2 Adapted from various sources

EX. 6 Adapted from: Time Life Books (1988) *Galaxies*, New York.

Unit 3

EX. 2 From: Crystal, D. (1997) *The Cambridge Encyclopedia of Language*, 2nd edition, Cambridge: Cambridge University Press, p. 88.

EX. 6 i) From: Nunan, D. (1988) *The Learner Centred Curriculum*, Cambridge: Cambridge University Press, pp. 32-33.

EX. 6 ii) From: Butterfield, C.H. (2003) 'The Effectiveness of Non-Governmental Organisations in Rural Poverty Alleviation in Uganda', Unpublished M.Sc. thesis (Institute for Development Policy and Management), University of Manchester, pp.11-13.

EX. 8b From: Lock, G. (1996) *Functional English Grammar: an introduction for second language teachers*, Cambridge: CUP, p.1.

Unit 4

EX. 3 From: Turk, J. and Turk, A. (1984) *Environmental Science*, 3rd edition, New York: CBS College Publishing, p. 42.

EX. 9 Adapted from various UNICEF sources

EX. 10 Adapted from: Baldwin, P.J., Dodd, M. and Wrate, R.M. (1997) 'Young doctors' health – II. Health and health behaviour' *Social Science and Medicine*, 45(1)41-44.

Unit 5

EX. 2 Adapted from: Fowles, J. (1994) 'Surface literacy, rooted orality: A hidden factor in teacher education in South Sulawesi'. Unpublished M.Ed. dissertation, University of Manchester, p.26.

EX. 10 Adapted from: Krashen, S. (1988) *Second Language Acquisition and Second Language Learning*, Prentice Hall: Hemel Hempstead, p.2.

Unit 6

EX. 2 Altbach, P.G. (2001) 'Academic Freedom: International realities and challenges', *Higher Education*, 41:205-219.

EX. 13 Adapted from: Clarke, D. (ed.) (1977) *A History of Inventions*, London: Cavendish.

Unit 7

EX. 1 Adapted from: Office of National Statistics (2005) *Social Trends*. www.statistics.gov.uk

EX. 2 Adapted from: Office of National Statistics (2005) *Social Trends*. www.statistics.gov.uk

EX. 5 Adapted from: Office of National Statistics (2005) *Social Trends*. www.statistics.gov.uk

EX. 6 Adapted from: Office of National Statistics (2005) *Social Trends*. www.statistics.gov.uk

EX. 8 Adapted from: Office of National Statistics (2005) *Social Trends*. www.statistics.gov.uk

EX. 12 **(graph)** Adapted from: Office of National Statistics (2005) *Social Trends*. www.statistics.gov.uk

EX. 12 **(reading)** Adapted from: Office of National Statistics (2005) *Social Trends*. www.statistics.gov.uk

EX. 14 Adapted from: Office of National Statistics (2005) *Social Trends*. www.statistics.gov.uk

EX. 16 Adapted from: Office of National Statistics (2005) *Social Trends*. www.statistics.gov.uk

Unit 8

EX. 2 From: Altbach, P.G. (1990) 'Impact and adjustment: foreign students in comparative perspective', *Higher Education* 21:305.

EX. 3 **(Introduction 1)** From an assignment written by a Manchester Management student

EX. 3 **(Introduction 2)** From an assignment written by a Manchester Landscape and Planning student

EX. 3 **(Introduction 3)** From an assignment written by a Manchester Development Studies student

EX. 6 From an assignment written by a University of Dublin Economics student

Unit 9

EX. 2 (also see Introduction 2b, Unit 8, p 65) Altbach, P.G. (2004) 'Higher education crosses borders'. *Change*. March-April, 1-2.

Cook, C. and Johnson, P. (2004) Issues to consider: Is study abroad the right choice for me? http://www.prospects.ac.uk/cms (correct on 29/06/04) np.

Dwyer, M. and Peters, C. (2004) 'The benefits of study abroad'. *Abroad View*. http://www.abroadviewmagazine.com/why_study_abrd/benefits.html (correct on 29/6/04) np.

Goodwin, C. D. and Nacht, M. (1988) *Abroad and beyond: Patterns in American overseas education*. Cambridge: Cambridge University Press.

Oberg, K. (1960) 'Cultural shock: Adjustment to new cultural environments'. *Practical Anthropology*. 7, 177-182.

UKCOSA (2003) 'International students and culture shock'. *UKCOSA Guidance Notes for Students*. http://www.ukcosa.org.uk/pages/guidenote.htm (correct on 29/06/04) np.

Unit 10

EX. 2 Adapted from: Webster, C.C. and Wilson, P.N. (1980) *Tropical Agriculture*, London: Longman, p.231.

EX. 5 From: Turk, J. and Turk, A. (1984) *Environmental Science*, 3rd Edition. New York: CBS College Publishing, p.98.

Unit 11

EX. 8 Adapted from: Rejabi, R (2002) 'An investigation into sagittal thoracic curvature in cyclists and non-cyclists', Unpublished PhD thesis (Musculoskeletal Research Group), University of Manchester, p. 72.

Unit 12

EX. 2 From: Montgomery, M. and Reid-Thomas, H. (1994) *Language and Social Life*, London: The British Council, p.25.

EX. 14 Adapted from: MacRae, F. (2005) 'The dieters destined for failure' *Daily Mail*, 2 December.

Unit 1

1 The topic sentence is d, and the sentence order in the original paragraph is: d, b, c, a.

3 i) The topic sentence is b, and the sentence order in the original paragraph is: b, d, c, a.

ii) The topic sentence is d, and the sentence order in the original paragraph is: d, a, c, b.

iii) The topic sentence is b, and the sentence order in the original paragraph is: b, d, c, a.

iv) The topic sentence is c, and the sentence order of the original paragraph is c, d, b, a.

Note: How good is c as a topic sentence? It is very general and does not introduce the main idea in the paragraph that cycling may be harmful to children.

4 There are three paragraphs in this text. Each paragraph begins with topic sentences which are as follows:
Line 1: Weather conditions in Arabia vary almost as much as the terrain.
Line 6: Temperature and humidity ranges are equally disparate.
Line 13: The climate of the peninsula, ...

5 i) Writers may give specific examples as evidence to support their general claims or arguments. Examples can also be used to help the reader understand unfamiliar or difficult concepts. For this reason, they are often used in teaching. Finally, students may be required to give examples in their work to demonstrate that they have understood a complex problem or concept.

Many paragraphs in academic writing show a development from the general to the specific. In most paragraphs, therefore, examples usually come after the topic sentence.

ii) Words like *gay, wicked, cool* have all acquired new meanings. Other examples include *launch pad,* and many words from computer science which have become part of the standard language e.g. *interface* and *default.*

Some of the above words have become more specialised in meaning; others have acquired a broader meaning.

6 The meaning of a word can change through **extension** – the widening of initial sense to cover other meanings – e.g. great
narrowing – limiting the meaning to a specific field – e.g. doctor

7
1 widen, broaden, extend	5 enjoyable
2 others	6 learned
3 example	7 used
4 great	

8 **The underlined words should be:** for example, – Another illustration is ... – A classic example ... – similar instances. – ... (are) cases in point –
Other words or phrases sometimes used to give examples are: ... like – ... similarly

9 Paragraph 1

Extension of meaning
Example 1: lovely/enthusiastic approval of a rather vague sort
Example 2: great/enthusiastic approval of a rather vague sort
Example 3: dean/senior person of any group or class

Paragraph 2

Narrowing of meaning
Example 1: doctor/medical doctor
Example 2: park/to leave a car
Example 3: tank/heavy armoured fighting vehicle

Narrowing of meaning (special vocabulary)
Example 1: enlargement/ large print made from a small negative (photography)
Example 2: senior/member of the graduating class (US education)
Example 3: gas/particular kind of gas (domestic kitchen)

Narrowing of meaning (local vocabulary)
Example 1: nickel/coin (US)
Example 2: prohibition/prohibition of alcohol (US)
Example 3: democrat/member of the Democratic Party (US)
Example 4: republican/member of the Republican Party (US)

The examples of special and local vocabulary are not introduced explicitly by phrases such as **for example**. This is particularly common in contexts where other examples have already been given.

11 *Such as* tends to be followed by nouns or noun phrases. *For example* can also be followed by nouns or noun phrases, but in academic writing it is often used to introduce a whole sentence.

(i) a) The desire to avoid stress may also lead people to avoid potentially beneficial changes to their lives, **such as** job changes and promotions.

b) Giving people the correct information can encourage them to adopt health promoting behaviour, **such as** cutting down on smoking and drinking.

c) People are more likely to pay attention to certain bodily sensations, **such as** aches and pains, when they are under stress.

d) The focus of medical care in our society has been shifting towards changing many of our unhealthy behaviours, **such as** poor eating habits, smoking and failure to exercise, rather than simply curing the resulting diseases.

e) For some people, being called upon to give a talk in front of a class is a highly stressful stimulus that will immediately produce symptoms of an alarm reaction, **such as** a pounding heart and a dry mouth.

f) Young people begin smoking for a variety of reasons, **such as** peer pressure and the role modelling of parents.

Note: **For example** could be used in the above sentences but may sound a little clumsy since we normally expect something more elaborate to follow.

(ii) a) **For example,** they may avoid changing jobs or fail to pursue promotion opportunities.

b) **For example,** once people are aware of the dangers of smoking and heavy drinking, they are more likely to cut down.

c) **For example,** aches and pains are often felt to be more serious than they really are.

d) **For example,** much more emphasis is now placed on healthy eating, not smoking and taking regular exercise.

e) It is not uncommon, **for example,** for speakers to experience a pounding heart and a dry mouth.

f) They may, **for example**, be influenced by their peers, or they may see their parents as role models.

Unit 2

3 1 makes   4 useful   7 essential
2 total   5 one   8 toxic
3 classifying   6 groups   9 non-essential

4 a) According to/On the basis of GNP, countries may be **classified/divided into** low-income countries, middle-income countries and high-income countries.

b) **On the basis of/According to** their physical appearance, human beings **may/can be divided/classified** into Negroids, Caucasians and Mongoloids.

c) **According to/On the basis of** age of study, the education system **may/can be divided/ classified into** the primary sector, the secondary sector and the tertiary sector.

d) **On the basis of/According to** whether they eat plants, other animals or both, animals **may/can be divided/ classified into** herbivores, carnivores and omnivores.

e) **According to/On the basis of** whether or not they shed their leaves seasonally, broad-leaved trees **may/can be divided/classified into** deciduous and evergreen trees.

f) **On the basis of/According to** their origin, rocks **can be divided/classified into** igneous rocks, sedimentary rocks and metamorphic rocks.

5 a) i) 1 may be divided into   3 such as/including
2 such as/including

ii) 4 may be divided into   6 such as/including
5 including

iii) 7 On the basis of

b) i) 1 main groups   4 third group
2 tiny   5 comprises
3 second category

ii) 6 On the basis of
7 divided into
8 further sub-divided into

6 d) Edwin Hubble's effort to classify the 'extragalactic nebulae', as he called galaxies, was a lifelong pursuit.

b) His scheme, published in 1936, is based on an examination of photographs taken by Mt Wilson's 1.5 and 4.5 meter telescopes.

f) As his collection of photographs grew, he modified the scheme but kept its essential features.

Paragraph break

e) Hubble divided galaxies into two broad types: regulars, which show rotational symmetry about a central nucleus, and irregulars which lack this symmetry, and thus were not included in this sequence.

a) Regular galaxies were divided into ellipticals and spirals.

g) Two branches of spirals – one with a bar across the nucleus – were classified according to the size of the nuclear region and the openness of the arms.

c) Other schemes have been developed, but Hubble's basic classification is still the most widely used.

Also possible is: d b e/a g f c

8 a) a) noun – formal
b) noun and verb – formal
c) noun – formal
d) verb – formal

e) verb – formal
f) noun – formal, neutral
g) noun and verb - informal
h) noun and verb – noun informal, verb formal and informal
i) verb, adjective – formal
j) noun, verb – noun formal, verb neutral and could be used in academic writing
k) verb – informal
l) noun, verb – formal

b) i) 1 classify/stereotype

ii) 2 category

iii) 3 stereotype

c) i) 1 grouping   2 distinction

ii) 3 selected   4 a set of

iii) 5 distinguish

9 a) i) 1 features
ii) 2 consequences
iii) 3 advantages

b) Words and phrases used for listing are –
i) One   Another
ii) firstly   secondly   thirdly   finally
iii) none. (three advantages)

c) i) 1 causes
ii) 2 elements
iii) 3 stages

d) i) two particular, one, the other
ii) three key; first; second; third
iii) three distinct; finally

11 a) Political parties in the Western political system have ideologies and political programmes. Their functions include the interests of society and they try to influence ruling bodies as well as trying to make citizens more politically active, recruiting candidates and forming governments.

b) Parents who want to reduce the risk of their teenagers using drugs, alcohol and tobacco should be aware of the three contributing factors. These are teenagers who may have too much stress in their lives, who do not have enough to do and who have too much spending money.

Unit 3

1 i) • To explain the exact meaning of a word or phrase. In academic writing students are often expected to give definitions of key words and phrases in order to demonstrate to their tutors that they understand these terms clearly. Academic writers generally, however, define terms so that their readers understand exactly what is meant when certain key terms are used in the context of a particular piece of writing.

• The kind of terms that need defining are key words or phrases in an assignment title; very technical, new or unfamiliar terms; and terms that have no standard, agreed definition.

• While dictionary definitions indicate the general meaning of a word, they are often too imprecise to be useful as academic definitions. Dictionary definitions should not be quoted as the 'authoritative' meaning of a term, for dictionaries do not confer meaning, but simply describe how words are used by speakers of a language.

- Because many concepts and ideas in academic writing are complex and controversial, different writers may interpret the same term in different ways: hence the need to clarify exactly what is meant by a particular term in a particular context. This means that definitions are often used by academic writers as part of their argument and that the definitions themselves may become the subject of further discussion or debate. When important terms are not clearly understood, misinterpretation may result. In fact, many disagreements (academic, legal, diplomatic, personal) arise as a result of different interpretations of the same term. In academic writing, teachers and their students often have to explore these differing interpretations before moving on to study a topic.

3 a) Most approaches begin by recognising the 'sentence', and grammar is thus most widely defined as the study of sentence structure.
   b) A grammar of a language, from this point of view, is an account of the language's possible sentence structures, organised according to certain general principles.
   c) Noam Chomsky (1928 -) writes that a grammar is a 'device of some sort for producing the sentences of the language under analysis' (1957, p. 11).
   Differences: a) has no relative clause, b) has a relative clause but the *which* has been dropped (often the case with passive constructions): this is termed a reduced relative clause, c) makes use of a prepositional phrase: *for producing*.

   Also: a) is the most general, c) is the most specific/exact.

4 a) university   e) Astronomy
   b) Research   f) Social
   c) World Wide Web   g) sentence
   d) noun   h) Palaeontology

Differences:

1 Use of articles: **a/an** is used before a term that is countable (definitions a, d, g); no article is used before a term that is uncountable (definitions b, e, f, h); **the** is used before a term that is specific or unique (definition c).
2 Verb forms: **is** is the main verb in six definitions (a, b, c, d, g, h); the use of **may be defined** in definitions f and h makes the definitions more cautious or tentative. The verb in the relative clause may be **active** (definitions b, h) or **passive** (definitions a, c, f, g). Definition d uses a modal verb (can).
3 Relative pronouns: **which** is used in definitions b, d, h; **which** preceded by a preposition is used in definition g; the relative pronoun is dropped (i.e. a reduced relative clause is used) in definitions c and f where the verb is passive.

   Typical structure: *A term* is *a general class/ category word + relative pronoun + distinguishing detail/characteristics.* A definition usually identifies the general class or category to which a term belongs and then differentiates the term from other members of the class.

   Definition h is an *extended* definition; the others are one-sentence definitions. An extended definition adds more information, e.g. by giving an explanation or example.

5 a) **An** electron **is an** elementary particle **assumed** to be a constituent of every atom.
   b) **An** antigen **is a** substance **which causes** the formation of antibodies, the body's natural response to foreign substances.
   c) **The** atmosphere **is** the gaseous envelope **which surrounds/surrounding** the Earth or other celestial body.
   d) Statistics **is/may be defined as** the branch of mathematics **concerned** with the collection, analysis, interpretation and presentation of masses of numerical data.
   e) Reliability **is a** measure of the consistency or reproducibility of data usually **determined** by the test-retest method, where ...
   f) **A** virus **is a** member of a group of sub-microscopic agents which **infect** plants and animals, usually manifesting their presence by causing disease.
   g) Grammar **is/may be defined as** a term **which refers/referring** to the study of the classes of words, their inflections and their functions and relations in a sentence.

6 i) **Differences:** this text not only introduces a definition, but also highlights a problem with the definition (academic definitions are rarely straightforward; they are often discussed critically). This text also indicates how the definitions have developed.

   Structures used to write about Chomsky's definitions:

   For Chomsky, 'competence' refers to ...
   Noam Chomsky writes that a grammar is a 'device of some sort for ...'

   Other ways of introducing other people's definitions: See section 7, p. 26.

   ii) There are ten definitions of poverty.

   Paragraph 1: 1) 'a lack of the minimum nutritional intake needed to sustain life' (the writer thinks this is inadequate cf. 'Our understanding of poverty has come a long way since ...'). **2) and 3)** 'Chambers et al. identify two senses of the word poverty ...i) a synonym for deprivation ... ii) what is measured in poverty assessment (the writer thinks these are relevant definitions cf 'the former helps understand poverty ... the latter is needed to give an overview of poverty ...'.

   Paragraph 2: Absolute/Relative poverty **1)** 'Absolute poverty occurs when ...' and **2)** 'An individual suffers from relative poverty when ...' (the writer thinks that these definitions are valid cf. 'A further distinction can be made between ... We must, however, recognise that poverty depends on the particular society').

   Paragraph 3: Traditional/More recent definitions **1)** 'traditional definitions, based on a narrow income/consumption view'; **2)** 'more recent definitions, which have broadened to include ...'; and **3)** 'The World Bank and other development actors now accept that poverty encompasses these, and other forms of deprivation, such as ...' (the writer agrees with these more recent definitions cf. 'This inclusion ... deepens our understanding of the realities of poverty').

   Paragraph 4: Transient/Chronic poverty **1)** 'The transient poor, who move in and out of poverty' and **2)** 'those in chronic poverty, i.e. those 'who either experience extended duration of poverty, or those who ...' (again the writer considers these definitions to be important cf. 'A final distinction deserves consideration here' ... 'A dynamic approach to defining poverty will therefore be more insightful').

Unit 4

1 Cause
a) Boredom at work
b) Local planning
c) The bad performance of large parts of Britain's manufacturing industry

Joining phrase
a) can lead to
b) can give rise to
c) was the cause of

Effect
a) low levels of productivity and high levels of absenteeism
b) an environment completely to their liking
c) Britain's relatively poor economic record at that period

2 Cause
a) Dutch Elm Disease
b) the larger number of learners and, a shortage of teachers in nurse education
c) reduced catches
reduced demand **_and_** increasing prices
d) population growth and large-scale destruction of forests by logging companies

Joining Phrase
a) owing to
b) owing to
c) due to, resulting from
d) resulting from, as a result of

Effect
a) more elm trees were cut down
b) medical schools are creating more courses based on learning by discovery, with the teacher acting as guide, counsellor and facilitator
c) reduced demand **_and_** increasing prices
the fall in the consumption of fish
d) ... serious erosion problems ...

The prepositional phrase 'owing to' fronts the cause, at the beginning of sentence b.
There is a chain of causes and effects beginning with 'reduced catches' in sentence c.
In Ex. 1, cause precedes effect; in Ex. 2, effect precedes cause – apart from 2b.

3

Causes	Results
Protein deficiency	mental retardation
Vitamin and mineral deficiency	weak bones, loss of teeth, blindness, or failure of any of a number of vital organs
Insufficient protein or calories	bloated bellies, thin arms and legs, wide eyes and shrivelled skin
Severe malnutrition	early and irreversible brain damage
Lack of Vitamin A	permanent blindness
Lack of iodine	deafness

4 Verb: result (+ in), lead (+ to), caused (+by)
Subordinator (before sub-clause): because
Preposition: owing to
Adverb (+ verb + -_ing_): thereby

They make the sentence less certain, and more cautious. In academic writing this is usually a good thing.

6 a) As a result   d) because, due
b) resulting   e) thereby
c) Consequently/As a result   f) resulting

7 a) gives rise   d) affected by
b) give rise   e) depends
c) caused   f) as a result

8 1 c   2 a   3 d   4 b

9 1 i) nutrition
ii) pollution
iii) affects children's body weight/resistance to disease.
iv) problems at school

2 i) attend school
ii) educated
iii) education
iv) employment
v) child poverty

3 i) exploitation, violence, abuse
ii) families
iii) cash grants
iv) rise in visits to clinics
v) under five deaths
vi) survival programme
vii) infant mortality

4 i) Elimination of child labour

5 i) Consult children
ii) targeting of education

10 prevalence   (line 4) – occurence
self-prescribe   (line 11) – treat themselves
confidential   (line 22) – private
stoicism   (line 22) – not complaining when ill

Paragraph 1:   a) Young doctors suffer from fairly frequent minor illnesses
b) Respiratory infections, mental health problems

Paragraph 2:   a) Self-prescription or colleagues prescribe
b) Future patterns of inappropriate behaviour, unlikely to seek appropriate health advice

Paragraph 3:   a) Not aware of, and/or do not use OHS, stoicism, storing up problems for future
b) Promotion of OHS, which must be accessible and confidential, alter climate of stoicism

Unit 5

2 While reading questions:
line 13: these = a few thousand words
line 16: This = accommodating the memory of the past to the reality of the present
line 33: that = that the way words are said may offer meanings

3 Paragraph 2:
Writing
1 freezes thoughts/ideas
2 reference across time and place
3 total number of words increases

Oral Language
1 a) restricted vocabulary
   b) vocabulary limited to concretions

Paragraph 3:
Oral Societies
1 a) past accommodated to present
   b) social situations harmonised
2 anchored in present
3 a) little idea of year of birth
   b) lives not ruled by clock

Literate Societies
1 Constraints of past
2 a) aware of time
   b) date and time in media
   c) date and time displayed in public places

Paragraph 4:
Orality
1 face-to-face may emphasise manner of speaking
2 meaning in context

Writing
1 communication over distance
2 a) need for punctuation
   b) need to be unambiguous
   c) need for complication and precision
3 meaning in the language

4 a) in contrast   c) instead of
    b) whereas/while   d) While/Whereas

5 a) However   c) In contrast to
    b) While   d) alternatively

7 a) Food eaten in northern Europe is quite different from that eaten in southern Europe.
    b) The survey suggests that the situation in Manchester is similar to that in Athens.
    c) The Arabic which is spoken in Morocco is very different from that (which is) spoken in Bahrain.
    d) Programmes on German television are quite similar to those on British television in a number of respects.
    e) The answers given by the students in Group A were not very different from those given by the students in Group B.
    f) The geological composition of the planet Mars is quite different to that of (the planet) Earth

10 The text follows pattern 1.

Unit 6

1 Pre-reading
Focus questions:
It is intrinsically interesting to trace the historical development of a particular problem, issue, theory or topic. But apart from this, the background information provides us with information which helps us to understand and explain why things are the way they are in the present. In other words, the past helps us to understand the present.

The background to a topic or issue is generally found in the early part of a text. In an essay, this would be after the introduction. How much we write about the background of a topic will, of course depend on the topic and the field of study. In science texts, background may be included as a very brief overview of previous significant research, and will tend to focus on the more recent developments. In the social sciences, past and/or more recent social, economic and political changes tend to be important. In the arts, social change and artistic tradition may both be important. And of course, in all fields, writers may take a purely historical perspective.

3 a) F   b) F   c) F   d) T   e) T   f) T

4 A situation which began in the past and continues to exist – present perfect

A situation which began in the past and came to an end in the past – past passive

6 undertook, fell, grew, put, spread, forecast, found, brought, raised, cost, began, upset, increased, rose

8 The inserted adverbial clause which refers to a specific time *(especially during the 1960s and 1970s ...)* does not determine the whole meaning of the main verb (to be), which, in the present perfect tense, still means ... *generally up to now*.

10 undertaken, fallen, grown, put, spread, forecast, found, brought, raised, cost, begun, upset, increased, risen

11 a) has been   f) challenged
     b) established   g) were
     c) were   h) made
     d) has been   i) have shown
     e) has been   j) grew

12 a) **Not only** do these findings provide new insights, **but they also** add further fuel to the controversies surrounding Heisenberg.
     b) **Not only** do the students conduct the psychoanalysis of at least three patients under the close and extended supervision of experienced psychoanalysts, **but they also** undergo a personal analysis.
     c) **Not only** do nanotubes conduct heat better than any other known material, **but** they are **also** about a hundred times stronger than steel.
     d) In this case, **not only** did subsequent experiments fail to reproduce the data, **but** a much more thorough analysis of the 1999 data failed to confirm the events.
     e) **Not only** is this project aimed at anticipating events in this region, **but** it is **also** designed to enhance our limited ability to discern and interpret signs of unrest in other volcanic areas.

13 d) to make – past perfect
     e) to produce – simple past – an action or event that took place at a specific time in the past
     f) to be described – simple past passive – a continuous state or situation at a known time in the past
     g) to hit upon – simple past – an action or event that took place at a specific time in the past
     h) to be (widely) distributed – simple past passive – a continuous state or situation at a known time in the past
     i) to improve upon – simple past – an action or event that took place at a specific time in the past
     j) to be attracted – simple past passive – a continuous state or situation at a known time in the past

k) to be translated – simple past passive – an action or event that took place at a specific time in the past

l) to become – past perfect – an action in the past which occurs before another action in the past or before a mentioned time (+ *by*)

14 a) It was Galileo **who** first saw the moons of Jupiter.
b) It was Bacon **who** improved upon al-Haytham's theories.
c) It is to take advantage of the lower production costs **that** multinationals invest in developing countries.
d) It is the greenhouse effect **that** is responsible for the recent changes in global warming.
e) It is the second part of your argument **that** is flawed.
f) It was through his work with the dreams of his patients **that** Jung developed his theory of the collective unconscious.
g) It was on the basis of their behaviour **that** the subjects were classified as being 'nice' or 'nasty'.
h) It is the overall balance in the diet **that** is important.
i) It is the second example cited in the text **that** provides us with a key to his character.

Unit 7

2 a) F   c) T   e) T   g) T
b) F   d) F   f) T

3 a) ii   c) v   e) i
b) iv   d) vi   f) iii

4 a) In 2003 there were 696,000 live births in the United Kingdom.
b) Births in 2003 were 36 per cent fewer than in 1901.
c) During the inter war years the number of births remained low.
d) In 1901 infant mortality accounted for 25 per cent of deaths (in 1901).
e) Developments in medicine help to explain the decline in death rates.
f) By the middle of the last century infant mortality had fallen to 4 per cent of deaths.

6 a) T   b) F   c) T   d) F   e) T

7 a) ii   c) i   e) iii
b) vi   d) iv   f) v

8 a) 4   b) 5   c) 2   d) 3   e) 1

11 a) It reached a low point in 1950.
b) Between 1960 and 1965, it rose dramatically.
c) It peaked/reached a peak in 1965.
d) It fell sharply between 1965 and 1970.
e) It remained level between 1980 and 1985.
f) There was a steady increase between 1990 and 2000.

12

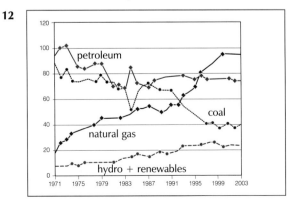

13 1 shows   4 peaked   7 projected
2 since   5 decreased   8 start
3 fall   6 fairly   9 deaths

14 a) vii   c) v   e) i   g) vi
b) iv   d) ii   f) viii   h) iii

15 It gives an explanation for the depletion in numbers.

2 Reading
There was a mini boom in births in the late 1980s and early 1990s, *the result of* the larger cohorts of women born in the 1960s.
Rising standards of living and developments in medical technology and practice *help to explain* the decline in death rates.

6 Reading
This growth *was partly a result of* the babies born in the post-war boom.

This latter increase *was partly a 'one-off' effect of* the Divorce Reform Act 1969.

8 Paragraph reconstruction
Much of this growth *can be accounted for by* the increase in births to cohabiting couples.

Unit 8

2 a) **context and importance**
- Higher education is increasingly international, and foreign students are among the most important and visible elements in internationalisation. There are over one million students studying outside the borders of their countries ...
- In fact, foreign students are at the centre of a complex network of international academic relationships ...
- the impact of foreign students on academic institutions and the impact of foreign study on the students as well as the policies relating to these key questions.

definition
- ... million students studying outside the borders of their countries

purpose
- Its purpose is to reflect on some of the most important generalizations of the available research literature.

overview
- This essay is concerned with several important aspects of the foreign student phenomenon; those relating to the flow of students from the Third World to the industrialised nations including the impact of foreign students on academic institutions and the impact of foreign study on the students as well as the policies relating to these key questions.

b) **context and importance**
- At present, about 2 million students worldwide study outside of their home countries, a number which is surely set to increase in the future.

overview
- This short essay will discuss the benefits and some of the 'costs' of overseas study.

3 **Introduction 1:** d, a, b, c, e
Introduction 2: d, a, e, b, c
Introduction 3: c, e, b, d, a

5
  a) Laser cutting technology for manufacturing processes has recently attracted growing interest.

  b) As a result of these rapid changes , however, the global environment is becoming seriously damaged.

  c) So far, however, the use of modal verbs for this purpose has received little/no serious attention.

  d) The purpose of this essay is to consider the benefits and some of the 'costs' of overseas study.

7
1	important	4	concern
2	data	5	consists of
3	purpose	6	followed

9 The following section summarises the main points of the essay: The financial costs of study abroad are usually very high and individuals may experience personal and emotional difficulties. In spite of this, increasing numbers of students are finding that the long-term career benefits together with opportunities to acquire new knowledge and experiences, and to gain proficiency in a second language, make the study abroad experience very worthwhile.

10 a) **Brief Summary – paragraph 1**
This paper **has given an account** of and the reasons for the widespread use of the English language in today's world. Resistance to the use of English and inherent problems with the language itself **were also examined, along with** some of its more advantageous features. Finally, proposals to make the language easier to learn and more internationally standardised **were discussed**.

  b) **Final comment – paragraph 2**
At present there are few other contenders for the status of an international lingua franca. Many other widely spoken languages have strengths, but few match the lexical hybridisation or the inflectional simplicity which give English such wide appeal. Furthermore, no other language has such a dominant role in commercial, diplomatic, scientific and technical fields as English does at the present time. **It seems, then,** that English, despite its weaknesses and some opposition, **will most probably continue to develop** as the international language of communication, ideally in a simplified and more standardised form, **in the foreseeable future**.

13
1	e	3	a	5	f	7	b
2	g	4	d	6	c		

Unit 9

2 **Benefits**
Main point 1:
a) limited opportunities for specialised study at home
b) prestige value of overseas degrees and advantages in local job markets
Main point 2:
a) an enriching, stimulating and life-changing experience
b) to gain experience of living independently and to make new friends from all round the world
Main point 3:
one of the best ways of improving proficiency in a second language

Costs
Main point 4: financial costs are very high
Main point 5:
a) students will probably experience homesickness
b) many students will probably experience culture shock

3 *The first sentence of this paragraph serves two functions. What are they?*
It links back to the previous sentence and it also introduces a new point.

What can you say about the position of 'also' in this sentence?
It is often placed between the subject of the sentence and the main verb (but after an auxiliary verb or verb to be).
Why does the writer use 'in fact' here?
To introduce more information which supports a previous point

What can you say about the position of 'for example' in this sentence?
After the verb 'to be' and between commas

Which reaction?
'a negative emotional reaction' mentioned in the previous sentence

4 a) iii/ii   c) i   e) iv/v
    b) vi   d) v   f) ii

5 a) iii/ii/iv   c) iv/ii   e) ii/iv
    b) vi   d) i   f) v

6 a) In fact   d) For example
    b) nevertheless   e) Consequently
    c) In contrast   f) Alternatively

7 Compare adverbial connectors + subject + verb with prepositions + noun phrase

8 a) iii   b) ii   c) iv   d) i

9 a) In terms of   c) On account of
    b) Instead of   d) According to

10 a) iii   b) iv   c) ii   d) i

11 a) In spite of   c) with regard to
    b) In the light of   d) In addition to

13 a) The other interesting finding was that the scientific corpus analysed in this study contained a much lower density of modal verbs than the large general English corpora studied by Evans (2001) and analysed by Morley (1998). *Introduce finding + comparison with previous research*

  b) This is undoubtedly because the range of modal meanings appropriately conveyed in science writing, and possibly in some other types of academic writing, is in some ways more restricted than in many other written varieties. *Explanation for finding*

  c) Nevertheless, the high frequencies of the modals verbs *may* and *can* in the scientific corpora compared with the two general English corpora are interesting exceptions. *Surprising/exceptional findings*

  d) There are probably certain uses of *may* and *can* that are characteristic of scientific and possibly other academic texts, while some of the meanings of *will, would, could,* and *should* are less appropriate in scientific writing than in some other kinds of written English. *Possible explanation/hypothesis*

14 a) ii   b) iv   c) iii   d) i

15 a) iii   b) iv   c) i   d) ii

16 a) A strong relationship between X and Y has been reported in the literature. 14d

  b) These findings of the current study are consistent with those of Smith and Jones (2001) who found ... 14a

c) In contrast to earlier findings, however, no evidence of X was detected. 15a

d) Contrary to expectations, this study did not find a significant difference between ... 15d

e) The reason for this is not clear but it may have something to do with ... 15b

f) It is therefore likely that such connections exist between ... 14b

g) From the above it can be concluded that ... 14c

h) Further studies on the current topic are therefore recommended. 15c

Unit 10

1 1 ploughing
2 harrowing: breaking up large pieces of soil
3 raking: loosening and levelling the soil before planting seeds or seedlings
4 planting
5 ripening: to grow fully, to be ready for harvesting, eating
6 harvesting
7 threshing: separating the grains from the rest of the rice plant
8 winnowing: separating the chaff (outer part of rice grain) from the grain.

3 *Suggested Answers*
i) The land is first flooded then thoroughly cultivated using oxen or buffaloes.
ii) The seedlings are transplanted into puddled fields.
iii) Weeds are usually controlled by pulling them out by hand.
iv) The water is gradually drained off to facilitate the ripening and harvesting of the crop.
v) In most places the rice is harvested by hand.
vi) The harvested crop is threshed and winnowed.

5 1 are first prepared
2 use
3 is first established
4 then drags
5 determines
6 then operates
7 is applied
8 are spread
9 is finally harvested
10 is then cleaned
11 milled
12 refortified
13 depends
14 are needed

8 A speaker or writer may choose to use the passive for one or more of the following reasons:
- The identity of the agent of the action is unknown.
- The speaker or writer avoids identifying the agent because they do not want to assign or accept responsibility.
- There is no need to mention the agent since this information is obvious from context, or unimportant. The focus is on the verb and its object.
- To avoid repetition of a particular subject.
- To achieve a more objective/scientific tone.
- To put emphasis on the agent of an action.

9 a) The degree programmes will be reorganised to fit the new modular courses.
b) Most metals can be machined into precise dimensions.
c) This year's Biennial Conference is going to be held at Nottingham University.
d) The research data should have been checked more thoroughly.
e) The information is then used to predict population change over time.
f) Impurities in water can/may be classified as suspended, colloidal or dissolved.

11 i) 1 Describing some of the main methods used in the discipline d)
2 Giving reasons why a particular method was adopted c)
3 Indicating sample size and characteristics a)
4 Indicating sequence b)

ii) 5 Indicating purpose f)
6 Indicating manner h)
7 Indicating tools or instruments used e)
8 Indicating problems or limitations g)

12 **carried out:** survey, experiment, interviews, research
conducted: survey, experiment, interviews, research
noted: results, responses, data
set up: experiment, interviews, apparatus
observed: subjects, experiment
tabulated: results, data, responses
interviewed: subjects
selected: subjects, data, responses
obtained: results, data, responses
recorded: results, responses, interviews
Some other procedural verbs are: reported, reviewed, evaluated ...

13 1 In an attempt
2 were carried out
3 Prior to
4 For the purpose of/Prior to
5 sources of error
6 several advantages
7 In order to
8 Once
9 carefully
10 then

Unit 11

1 **N.B.** This task aims only to introduce some of the basic concepts of referencing, all of which will be dealt with in greater detail in the rest of the unit.

i) In examples a), b), and d) the name of the author of the original source and the date of publication of the original source are given in brackets at the end of the sentence.

In examples a) c), e), f), and h) the name of the author of the original source is the subject of the sentence, and, except for h) is followed by the date of publication of the original source in brackets. Example h) is using a footnote system for references. See **2. Reference systems used in academic writing.**

Example g) gives neither the original author nor the date, as a different system of referencing is being used. See **2. Reference systems used in academic writing.**

ii) & iii)

No.	Reporting Verb	Tense
a)	pointed to	simple past
b)	none	none
c)	none	none
d)	has indicated	present perfect
e)	found	simple past
f)	shows	simple present
g)	has been shown	present perfect passive
h)	writes	simple present

No.	Comment
a)	ideas no longer current
b)	focus on information
c)	single study
d)	reference to area of enquiry
e)	single study
f)	current knowledge
g)	current relevance/focus on information
h)	current interest/relevance

3 Examples 1), 3), and 5) are *information* prominent: the names of the source authors are given in brackets at the end of the sentence.

Examples 2) and 4) are *author* prominent: the name of the source authors are the subjects of the sentences.

N.B. In example 3) 'several authors' is the subject of the sentence and this could be called 'weak author prominent'. It seems simpler, however, only to distinguish author/information prominent as above.

In the **Introductory task**, examples b), d), and g) are *information* prominent; examples a), c) e), f) and h) are *author* prominent.

4 **First group:** argue c); mention b); conclude e); point out a); suggest d).
Second group: claim b); show d); maintain a); state e); identify c).
The two verbs which tend to be followed by a noun or noun phrase are 'identify' and 'mention'.

5 i) **Group 1 description:** identify, list, mention, point out
Group 2 opinion: claim, maintain, argue, suggest, conclude

ii) **Group 1:** Other verbs include: state, show, explain, indicate, note, describe, define, observe, comment.
Group 2: Other verbs include: assume, doubt, agree, interpret, believe, contend.

iii) a) Maynard (1993: 137) <u>lists</u> three reasons why the English language has become so dominant ...

b) Malawi (1999: 32) <u>maintains</u> that many heart attacks could be avoided with very limited changes in exercises and eating habits.

c) Popper and Friedman (1991: 77) <u>identify</u> poor food, bad housing, inadequate hygiene and large families as being the major causes of infant mortality.

d) Armani (1983: 72) <u>points out</u> that gardening has always been an effective therapy for those with depressive tendencies.

e) Sargnagel (1993: 20) <u>argues</u> that when a mother tongue is banned from the classroom the teaching tends to lead to the alienation of the students.

f) Carrow *et al.* (1990: 32) <u>conclude</u> that although curative medicine has ensured great health improvements in developing countries, preventative medicine is far more cost effective and therefore better adapted to the developing world.

g) Carter (1981:99) <u>mentions</u> the great Persian poet, Rumi as a comparison.

h) Bastien (1998: 67) <u>claims</u> that a range of illnesses can be diagnosed and treated by analysing the colour of the eye.

6 i) tense: mainly used in the past simple tense structure: not normally followed by that (*find* and *report* are exceptions) meaning: these are verbs of academic activity rather than exposition or opinion

ii) Other verbs include: demonstrate, measure, compare, observe.

iii) a) found/reported
b) analysed/studied/examined
c) examined/studied/analysed
d) reported/found/tested
e) reviewed

f) surveyed
g) studied/investigated

7 a) Example I + b + iii
Example II + c + i
Example III + a + ii

b) Example I + c + ii
Example II + a + iii
Example III + b + i

9 a) have indicated/indicate
b) found
c) are
d) argues/argued/has argued
e) has been widely investigated
f) is
g) studied
h) has been demonstrated
i) highlights/highlighted/has highlighted

11 Reference to what other writers do in their text; author as subject D
General descriptions of the relevant literature E
Reference to current state of knowledge G
Reference to single investigations in the past: investigation prominent C
General reference to previous studies/research A
Reference to single investigations in the past: research topic as subject F
Reference to single investigations in the past: researcher as sentence subject B

Unit 12

3 a) F   b) T   c) T   d) T   e) T

4 With reference to the research reported in paragraph 1:

i) No evidence is given for the Amsterdam research, only the conclusion. The key evidence in the Fishman study is given on lines 4-7 and 8-11.

ii) The evidence in the Fishman study is clearly relevant. More information could have been given, however, about how the couples were selected, how old they were, and how the conversations were recorded e.g. did the couples know that they were being recorded? If they were aware of being recorded, how much did this influence their conversations? Evidence from only three couples does not seem sufficient to draw conclusions about the use of questions by men and women in general.

iii) The sources given are presumably reputable, and were reasonably up-to-date at the time of writing (1994), although this would not be the case now.

iv&v) Fishman's interpretation of the evidence is questioned in Paragraph 2, which raises the possibility of a different conclusion.

vi) See ii) above.

vii) The statistics and data seem valid, but as stated in Paragraph 2, the data could have been further refined and more precise.

viii) There is no information in the text to suggest a possible bias.

5 a) However, ... no attempt to ...(line 13).
b) her conclusions would have been more persuasive if she had discussed in more detail ... (lines 16-18)

6 a) It would have been better if she had discussed the different types of questions.
The findings would have been more convincing if she had discussed the different types of questions.
The results would have been more useful if she had discussed the different types of questions.

b) No possibility of change: past conditional
Possibility of change: present conditional

d) a strong criticism
as much a suggestion as a criticism
a tentative suggestion

7 a flaw or weakness in some previous research
a flaw or weakness in some conclusions based on argument/evidence
a knowledge gap
a weakness with a plan or project or idea

8 a) ii   b) iii   c) iv   d) i

9 a) ii   b) iii   c) i   d) iv

11 **Negative:** limited, modest, small scale, flawed, simple
Neutral: small scale, simple, preliminary, exploratory, modest
Positive: important, innovative, original, rigorous, impressive, useful, interesting, ambitious

14 1 The research report has many weaknesses (if it is considered as an academic, rather than a newspaper, report). They include:
- The evidence lacks detail and precision e.g. paragraphs 4, 10, 11.
- Much essential information is not given e.g. paragraph 4 (*How much do levels of leptin fall?*); 10 (*How many healthy volunteers? How were they selected? How old were they?*) 11 (*How much leptin were they given? How? When?*).
- No published, dated sources for the research are given.
- As the report mainly concentrates on conclusions rather than detailed evidence, methodology etc., it is difficult to judge whether the evidence is interpreted correctly.
- The main conclusion in paragraph 2 is too general ('It's all because of our hormones').
- The final conclusion in paragraph 15 does not follow from the evidence in paragraphs 13 and 14: ('losing just an hour or two of sleep might be enough' ... / 'are at very high risk of becoming obese')
- The report lacks detailed data and few statistics are given.
- The research has been funded by a pharmaceutical company, which might indicate some bias.

2 Academic writing aims to be formal, precise, impersonal and objective.

Principal features of academic writing style include:
- The avoidance of slang or very colloquial expressions (because by definition these belong to the spoken rather than the written language)
- The use of precise, formal vocabulary e.g. *fifty-four multigenerational families living in the largely urban Delaware valley were included in the study.*
- The avoidance of contracted forms e.g. *can't, isn't.* These should be written in full.

- The avoidance of the first and second person e.g. *I, we, you, my, our, your* (because these are too personal). In some academic disciplines, however, such personal pronouns are more acceptable.
- The use of impersonal expressions e.g. *it can be concluded that*
- A greater use of passive verb forms than in less formal English e.g. *a survey was conducted*
- The use of hedging expressions to avoid claiming certainty e.g. *poverty tends to be more prevalent in Africa; drunkenness may be the cause of many road accidents.*

3 Differences from a typical academic text include:
- The use of short, mostly one-sentence, paragraphs.
- The use of mainly short sentences, which lack the complexity associated with academic text.
- The lack of referencing and sources.
- The use of the first person e.g. *we, our.*
- The use of contracted forms e.g. *it's, won't.*
- The use of rather informal vocabulary e.g. *could pave the way for, a significant dip in the levels.*
- The use of the dash, and the use of quotation marks across paragraphs e.g. paragraphs 8-9.
- The overall structure of the text is non-academic: for example, the main conclusion is given first, rather than last.

N.B. It should be noted that the purpose, style, and readership of a newspaper article are quite different from those of an academic article. Many features which would be unacceptable in academic writing are appropriate in a newspaper.